GRACE TO RECOVER

How to Divorce Hurt, Addiction and OVERCOME Trials with the Power of a Loving God

SHIRLEY D. LATOUR
& 10 Overcoming Women

DEDICATION

This book is dedicated to YOU, the many women and men who will brave the pages of this anthology to find a glimmer of hope. It is for you we wrote these words of how God graced us to recover through life's gym workout. You know, the sweat drops, tears shed, pain intensified and sometimes-even bloodshed in the "gym" of life.

It is also dedicated to everyone who had our backs through the years; and, to the naysayer, the people who said we'd never amount to anything or we aren't good enough, we thank you for making us prove our own self-worth to ourselves, to stand in the grace we were given by God himself. THANK YOU!

ACKNOWLEDGMENTS

To: TAMMIE MALDONADO, SHARON FINNEY, CANDY MOSES, TAYLOR STEPHENS, NOVICE MCDANIEL, Dr. MONICA DEBRO, ROXANNE ROBINSON, SANDI JOHNSON, SHONDA CURB and TRUENICE BRYANT-SHAW:

I want first to say Glory to God on High and BRAVO to you ladies!! To each and every woman who shared the love of Jesus Christ through her story on these pages, I Salute you. The strength and determination you displayed in your life's journey and willingness to obey the leading of the Holy Spirit in writing these short testimonies will impact MANY around the world. I THANK YOU for helping make this God project possible! I honor you for honoring me. I am eternally grateful, without you it would not have been possible!

TO: ARTINA NUCKOLLS, my assistant I drug along in my madness! THANK YOU, Queen for keeping me straight and encouraging me!

DAMITA C. SULLIVAN, What can I say about you? You have TRULY been a FRIEND and words are not enough to show you my gratitude to and for you! And the Foreword: RIGHT ON!!

To my children, Travon and Welina: you are my inspiration and reason for continuing to push forward in life. I thank you for being the GREATEST young people any mother could hope for! You were truly my light in those hours when I saw none. I love you both very much and to you I leave my legacy!!

FOREWORD

All I can say is, "WOW!" Life is a divine blessed gift that we get to receive and live. However, there are times when that very gift seems to be filled with curses that never originated with us, yet carry us on a course or path of destruction, that is conspired by the enemy of our souls...Satan.

In her collaboration, Author Shirley LaTour, as well as the other authors, transparently share with us the real struggles of their lives that had the potential to take them down a dark course of destruction and demise. YET, through faith in the divine hand and power of Almighty GOD, they were delivered through, out of, and from the diabolical plots, plans, and ploys of Satan to destroy them, to a life of blessing, prosperity, and success.

As you read this book, allow the love of our Heavenly Father to consume your very being and bring deliverance to your own soul through the powerful stories and testimonies of these authors.

Damita C. Sullivan
Founder
Dimensions of Love Outreach Ministries, Inc

CONTENTS

INTRODUCTION

Have you ever been left holding your broken heart? Can't uncover the root of a problem? Perplexed and looking for a solution when life takes an unexpected turn?

Discover how a gracious, loving, caring God stepped into our fallen world to redeem it. He sees your addiction, poor choices and hopelessness. Maybe you've been wounded by divorce or suffered as a result of domestic violence. Do you wonder how you'll care for your children, and yourself, now that you're facing the world alone?

No matter where you start, you can move forward one step at a time.

As a former first lady of a church, I've weathered many adversities in life and ministry. I know how the enemy of our souls, satan, tries all he can to destroy us so that we never fulfill our purpose in this life. I stand victorious over everything hurtled against me. I want you to know that you can recover. You can make it!

I've linked arms with other victorious women willing to be transparent and impart the wisdom it took years for them to achieve. If you open your heart and mind to receive what Christ has for you, you will overcome your challenges, discover your purpose, and live a better life this side of heaven!

Don't be the person who misses out on all that life has to offer. It might look bleak right now. You may be overwhelmed as you look at your losses. Yes, weeping may last for a night, but daybreak is coming. A better life is about to dawn.

You are moments away from discovering a true, living God who cares about every detail of your life. He wants to comfort you. But more than that, He wants to change you. Embrace your healing and recovery. Then, like these victorious women, turn around and be an instrument in someone else's healing.

It's a wonderful journey. Go ahead and take your life back. Flip the page and take your first step!

ADDICTION

"Addiction is a psychological and physical inability to stop consuming a chemical, drug, activity, or substance, even though it is causing psychological and physical harm."

Felman, A. (2018, October 26). "What is addiction?" *Medical News Today*. Retrieved from https://www.medicalnewstoday.com/articles/323465.php.

1

PORNOGRAPHY: A CERTAIN TRAP, OH BUT GRACE

Shirley D. LaTour

*W*e live in a world where anything goes. Traps are laid out for the young and "seasoned" alike. Pornography is such a rampant "activity" amongst not just those whom some would think of as having a dirty mind; the pimp, the prostitute, the drug dealer, the "dirty old man" next door, etc. You know, the stereotypical words used loosely. Pornography plaques our youth who are really just curious, college students, married men and women, the rich and the poor, the elderly and dare I say it, CHURCH FOLKS, to INCLUDE: The Pastor,

Teacher, Evangelist, Apostle and Prophet. Yes, the five-fold ministry is affected by pornography as well. How do I know? Well allow the foundation to be laid.

Pornography Roots

Pornography, according to Merriam Webster, is "the depiction of erotic behavior (as in pictures or writing) intended to cause sexual excitement; material (such as books or a photograph) that depicts erotic behavior and is intended to cause sexual excitement; or, the depiction of acts in a sensational manner so as to arouse a quick intense emotional reaction".

This word stems from the Greek word, *pornographos* ("writing about prostitutes") and since the 1950s has also taken on a non-sexual connotation: anything that piques the curiosity and elicits a response; for example, seeing violence on television.

Our televisions are saturated with images that "pique" our interest. For example, commercials after a short stretch of a sitcom or other show depicting the juiciest of burgers causes us to salivate and want to ingest even more though we just demolished a plate.

Cartoons nowadays are filled with adult topics and characters as a ploy to engulf the minds of our children. Women are exploited on a daily basis all to sell a car or even a pack of cigarettes. Late night television shows were once meant to air at night to keep our innocent children from seeing "adult TV" but now it is found all during the day and on almost every channel.

Video games are placed in the hands of our children (and adults) as a means of keeping them entertained and quiet but the depictions on some of these games are gruesome, violent, and/or sexual in nature; not to mention the music played to keep the player in a trance during play. Access to the Internet is freely gained on every devise; cell phones, tablets, laptops, etc. and lives are put in harm's way, unknowingly and knowingly. So, what does all this have to do with your life?

Pornography has deep roots and once it enters one's mind, it begins to alter perceptions. What was once off limits becomes accessible and desirable. The visual "flashbacks" in the mind begin to cause people to want to act out what is seen in the mind's eye. It causes one to want more of the fantasy, to be aroused more and more. It then causes a person to become dissatisfied with the norm and now there is thrill seeking on every level, for the next "high."

This is how people become addicted not just to pornography, but also to anything. The brain and body say MORE and the flesh wants to be pleased. What one at one time said they would never do now finds themselves doing that very thing. Paul puts it this way in Romans 7:14-16 MSG:

I can anticipate the response that is coming: "I know that all God's commands are spiritual, but I'm not. Isn't this also your experience?" Yes. I'm full of myself—after all, I've spent a long time in sin's prison. What I don't understand about myself is that I decide one way, but then I act another, doing things I absolutely despise. So, if I can't be trusted to figure out what is best for myself and then do it, it becomes obvious that God's command is necessary.

I certainly couldn't be trusted with my life and made some really ignorant decisions. Remember these verses of scripture as we delve in TOGETHER to discover what pornography causes and how those chains can be broken over our lives. Allow me to tell you how I became addicted to "pornography"; let's dive right in!

Where It All Began

'Twas the night before Christmas and all through the house, not a creature was stirring…except Shirley. See, I was a quiet, shy, reserved but very curious and adventurous child in many respects. Reading, writing and arithmetic, literally, were my loves.

The answers I wanted to know were not easily found at home and it wasn't easy, rather, it was impossible, to talk to either of my parents on the subject of sex. Wanting to know all there was to learn about life and how things worked, I searched in books and asked friends because I knew I couldn't go ask the "Holy Rollers".

This "wanting to know" led to listening to friends and being pressured into having sex at an early age; it wasn't that I necessarily wanted to be sexually active in high school, but I wanted to "fit in" as the other girls told of their experiences. I wanted to have some input as well and not feel like the lone wolf so at the age of 15, I gave up my virginity. (I've heard people say they lost their virginity but no boo, if you did it willingly with someone of your age, you GAVE away that most prized possession.)

Then it happened: a few of my classmates got pregnant junior year, most at 16 or 17. I saw their struggle to stay in school, still get good grades, take care of their child, and even saw some of their personal support systems or serious lack thereof.

From that point at 17, I decided I would no longer be sexually active while in school, first off because I knew my father would kill "him" and mother may put me out; secondly, I didn't want that struggle I saw with my friends; thirdly, I wanted to go to college and knew that would be a hard road. There was already enough madness in the house I did not want to be a part of, so I was "planning my escape" senior year.

"Oh happy, lucky day!" I thought to myself as the Army Recruiter came to my high school. You see? There was domestic violence at home. Mom and dad fought (verbally AND physically) all the time, there was child abuse to some of us children (six of us in all), and police were a REGULAR at 423…the terrible thing? They were Pastors living one way in front of others but at home there was mayhem. Needless to say, the recruiter's presence was a God sent and just what I needed to get out of there.

I left home in Indiana 10 days after graduation from high school, first permanent duty station: Korea December 1997. Met the guy of my dreams, beautiful relationship as friends first but then it happened, that evening came. The evening things heated up and it was decision time of whether or not to go all the way. I plainly felt the nudge of God, but I ignored that "warning". Have you ever done that, ignored a warning and continued to do something your way?

See, I had given my life to Christ at the age of 12. I had always been a different child, but I allowed myself to succumb to the pressures of this world during those years as a teenager. No guidance at home for a set apart life as a teenage Christian, just religion…

Six months of bliss then turned a steep corner and my world changed forever. I was pregnant at 18, about to turn 19. I was already in the Army and taking care of myself per say but pregnancy was a blow to my plans. On top of that, I never would have thought this guy would abandon me. Allow me to clarify: he broke up with me a week BEFORE I found out I was pregnant.

He was my best friend, lover and my world…mistake number ONE: placing others before God. I had clearly violated the commandment in Exodus 20:3 that says we should not have any gods before Him; therefore, consequences came with it. This led to a deep depression and even suicidal thoughts.

Seeds Planted and Began to Take Root

Back in 1998, Soldiers were not allowed to deliver their babies in Korea due to standards of care and they were not able to handle high-risk pregnancies. There were provisions or exceptions for some to stay there but I did not meet those criteria as a young, single Soldier; consequently, I was sent back to the states Oct 6, 1998 while the dad remained in Korea.

Next duty station: Fort Carson, CO, arrived October 26, 1998.

I mustered the strength to show up every day for duty, but I cannot say I was "there" in mind. My son was born on January 1, 1999 and I made myself a promise that I would never go back home but I would take care of my child no matter what. I was back attending church and had rededicated my life back to Christ as of February 15,1999. Six months passed, putting one foot in front of the other then another blow: he got married to someone else. How was he not ready to be a dad but ready to be a husband? This news sent me "over the edge" if you will.

My child's caregiver was an older woman in my church; however, she didn't know what I was going through because I was a very private person. I kept my pain bottled up, pushed down with the corkscrew on tightly but it began to fester. I needed an outlet, a soothing mechanism then a man appeared (that is usually when temptation appears, when we are the weakest). Actually, he was one of the ministers of music in my church and much older than myself. For a while even before the news of my son's dad getting married, this man tried to get next to me, but I wasn't having it until THE NEWS.

It was no holds bar from that point forward: anything and everything went. He wasn't even my type but the need to be comforted was greater. I started using sex to fill a void and a deep wound. Heck, I even had a willing participant in my folly, so I used an excuse like, "at least I'm only sleeping with one person and I'm not out in the streets" (rationalization). Have you ever made an excuse like that?

Trust me I'm not condemning you, I did it too, but I want you to be better and do better than I did. Hurt, pain and despair have a way of disguising itself but it has some lingering consequences, sometimes unseen until something catastrophic occurs. Do something DIFFERENT and I'll show you why.

That foothold became a stronghold QUICKLY. I recall the night I was on Staff Duty and I was introduced to porn by videotape. Someone in the barracks had it at the desk and I watched it that night. The seed was planted much earlier in my life and so with watching those acts, it took root and grew rapidly out of control.

Sex became my drug of choice. I wanted it daily, needed it daily, usually multiple times a day: it became an addiction. Between watching porn on HBO, Cinemax (Sin to the Max), videos, adult stores and acting it out, this vicious cycle of sin, repentance, sin, repentance continued for two years.

All the while, "the Minister" and I were in the same church serving in the choir and praise team, I was even the Hospitality President (serving up anything but God...). Sitting in service undressing the Man of God, just waiting to get home and get "that knock". To look back on it, I am grateful to have had a willing "partner in crime" or else I may have been on the street looking for a fix. All the same though: he was, it was an addiction that led to a whole lot more hurt, depression and loss.

Time to Move: The Army Said So

By this time, I was a month shy of 22, my son was about two and a half and it was time to move on to another duty station: Hawaii April 2001. The move across the water to a place where I knew no one and had a toddler to take care of but was barely grown myself, was overwhelming, to say the least. Not to mention that I had to leave the "comfort" of a familiar spirit, but that didn't last long.

He would travel on some weekends all the way to Hawaii to see my son and I and before long, I found myself doing the next DUMBEST thing in life: I asked this man to marry me, a much older man mind you…mistake number TWO: twisting scripture to fit what we (think) we want. The bible pronounces in Proverbs 18:22 that "The man who finds a wife finds a treasure, and he receives favor from the Lord." (NLT) The Bible is CLEAR on its instructions for our lives and when we veer from those instructions, chaos, and disorder and downright dysfunction ensue.

"What in the world was wrong with you?" you chuckle as you SYH (shake your head). Strongholds, stupidity (rather I was young and naïve), fear, doubt and downright desperation are the words that come to mind. It all stemmed from that previous rejection from someone I truly loved, and thought loved me in return.

I was going to hold on to this one no matter what. I was

lonely, had no self-esteem or self-worth and I felt unloved. I didn't understand what I had gotten myself into though. Wrappers are shiny and without wrinkles, but the insides are filled with unexpected things...

Shiny Wrappers with Unexpected Insides

Married in August 2001 with a toddler at 22, in the Army Soldiering away as a combat medic, working 24-hour shifts at points and 12-hour night shifts for a nine-month stretch proved to be more than I bargained for.

Within six months of our marriage, he had already been cheating on me with a female in the church we were attending. The nights I was away from home on duty he took the liberty to sleep around. He was certainly getting his fill at home so why was he doing this?

I gave him all I had in every area but that wasn't enough. What I didn't understand at the time was that he had an addiction to sex and pornography as well: yes-SHARED demons.

So much happened during that marriage including multiple infidelities on his part, control issues, wanting me to worship him above God, sexual abuse, amongst other things. That is not to say I was or am perfect; I certainly had faults too, but I honored my marriage vows to him and God even in those times.

It took a great toll on my spiritual, physical and mental wellbeing and eventually my physical safety.

The demons that had evolved, matured and manifested themselves at home were GREAT. I now know that the issues in my marriage stemmed from past sexual impurities and it started well before we met each other.

Sexual impurities of the past that have not been repented for (and present ones done in the dark) is how and why many church leaders, to include Bishops and Pastors, are caught up in sex scandals that are now spewed on national news. It can also be the determinant of why the divorce rate amongst Christians is equal to, if not greater than, non-Christians.

Getting Knowledge and Wisdom

Another change of duty station occurred in 2008 and in June 2010, the Mister had become a Pastor to a brand-new start up church. After having had enough of hurt, pain and downright misery and not finding the answers in the Word of God (I was so entangled, snared at the time, I could NOT hear the voice of God, but I knew He was still there), in December 2013 I went to the Christian bookstore and started searching for books on Godly marriage.

I found the answer I had been searching for all that time of why my marriage had gotten so out of hand: marriage does NOT fix your past sexual sins. You have to repent of those things even if you marry that same person you were in a fornication or adulterous relationship with.

Please hear me: REPENT of your sin; don't marry just to cover the sin. Repent, both of you, TOGETHER. No, really, ask God to forgive you, be sincere about it and STOP sinning against your own body and God.

The Holy Spirit will help you, but you have to let Him in and allow him full control of our life! If your partner refuses to repent before marriage, RUN the other way, you still have time and a way of escape. If you are married and you repent but your partner refuses to repent, dear sir/madam, buckle up for the ride. (No space to explain now but pick up my next book!)

The scripture in 1 Corinthians 7: 9 that utters it is better to marry than to burn is many times taken out of context. It says in its entirety, "But if they can't control themselves, they should go ahead and marry. It's better to marry than to burn with lust." (NLT)

We certainly couldn't control ourselves in our sin nature. The truth is that we were two very broken individuals trying to comfort ourselves, mask hurt instead of addressing the roots of our pain that stemmed from childhood and/or early adulthood. Those roots resurfaced in marriage and I can tell you, NOT in a good way, BUT GOD!!

Points to Ponder and Act Upon

1. Pornography cannot be overcome by natural means because it is a spiritual battle. I had to go to God and ask for forgiveness of every sin I had committed, specifically those sexual sins. Up until the point of my repentance in December 2013, every sexual encounter with my husband I literally felt like another woman. Then and only then did I feel like Shirley again and was able to relate to and enjoy sex as myself in a right relationship (from my standpoint with God anyway).

2. Sex is a beautiful thing and God designed it, so it is GOOD; HOWEVER, only within the confines of marriage. These "rules" were placed by God only to protect us. He knew the damage and hardships it would cause outside of covenant. These words were uttered in Hebrews 13:4 *"Marriage should be honored by all, and the marriage bed kept pure, for God will judge the adulterer and all the sexually immoral" (NIV)*.

3. You can overcome the addiction of pornography and everything that binds you as a consequence of it. Be sincere in your prayers. God hears you and He will answer. He did it for me! He broke every chain holding me so that I could be who He had ordained me to be, even from the foundation of the world!

4. You must have a personal relationship with Christ in

order to get and stay free of addictions and anything that holds you captive. Know that the Word of God is true and speak His Word over your life.

For anyone reading this chapter and you don't know Jesus personally, allow me to lead you to the cross of Jesus Christ. Yielding my will to His made ALL the difference in the world. He fights my battles for me and will for you too. He truly sets free! Repeat this prayer out loud:

Dear Heavenly Father, I come to you today by way of Jesus. I confess all of my sins to you this day, forgive me. I know that I cannot do this life alone and believe You are the answer! I believe in my heart that Jesus is Lord and that You God raised Jesus from the dead. I ask that you fill me with the gift of the Holy Spirit to lead and guide me through this life's journey. Thank you for coming into my life today and making my life brand new. Amen.

If you prayed this prayer and believe it by faith, you are now saved! The next steps are to get to a local church and learn as much as you can about Jesus because you will be tested and tried, I can assure you. Get a Holy Bible from the store and even download one on your devise. READ, READ, READ it! He will guide you. Get around other believers of Christ.

There is so much I could say on this topic that cannot be written here so stayed tuned for the book I will bring on this topic alone. Just remember that just because people are in church and in leadership positions, it doesn't mean they are above sinning. *For everyone has sinned; we all fall short of God's glorious standard. Romans 3:23 (NLT)* We are humans just like anyone else so pray for us. We all have a choice to make.

2

FREEDOM OUT OF BROKENNESS

Tammie Maldonado

This story that I'm about to share is only a glimpse at how God's Amazing Grace has taken me from a life of addiction, brokenness and chaos and restored me back to wholeness. According to the plan of the enemy and the world, I shouldn't have the courage to share what I'm about to. God says differently, and today I'm here to tell you that His POWER will break any chains that may have you in bondage.

I was born and raised in California in a town called

Bakersfield. When people tend to think of California, they picture palm trees, beaches, Hollywood and movie stars. Where I'm from is far from that. It's a valley right in the middle of the state. A lot of people I know back home haven't seen outside the Eastside of our town let alone a beach or a movie star! Drugs and violence run rampant through my hometown. Methamphetamine is a plague there that continues to breed darkness.

My parents divorced when I was eight years old. I have one brother who is four years younger than me and we have a half-brother on our dad's side who is quite a few years younger than us. My brother and I were raised together by our mother.

I remember the night clearly that my mother left my father. In fact, it's one of the very few memories I have of my childhood. We had moved to a town called Simi Valley in southern California because my father's job transferred us there. We had only been there a few months when one night I was spending the night at a friend's and my mother came and picked me up in the middle of the night.

She had my brother in the back seat and we drove straight to the police station. She took us into the police station with her but before doing so she reached into the glove compartment and pulled out a gun. I remember she went

19

up to the desk and told the woman working that my father was home drunk, and she was leaving him.

She told the lady the gun belonged to my dad and she wanted to turn it in. The police then escorted us back to our house where my mom gathered our clothes and we left to head back to Bakersfield. I remember clearly screaming and yelling and wanting my dad. Even though I had never as much seen my parents argue, I knew at that moment that we were never going to live together again. It's crazy as I think back, I know something broke inside me that night.

My mother was a nursing assistant. As soon as we were in Bakersfield a few days, she received a job in a local nursing home and began to work forty plus hours a week to support us. We lived with my grandmother, grandfather, (who died shortly after we moved in) and my uncle who was four years older than me. My mother worked, and my grandmother took care of us.

The house was nice on the outside and even beautiful on the inside but the dysfunction that was behind those doors was another story. Over the last few years, the secrets that were hidden deep in those walls have started to come to light. The saying, "Unhealthy people create unhealthy people" is absolutely true.

When I was thirteen, we moved out of my grandmothers and into an apartment of our own. By this time, I was already sexually active, drinking alcohol and smoking marijuana. My brother and I pretty much watched ourselves because our mother worked. She would leave before we went to school and she would come home about three hours after us.

There wasn't much communication at all between my mother and I except in the form of screaming and yelling. My mother was bitter and resented my father for the divorce. She worked very hard to provide for us and I have to admit I went against her every step of the way.

Over the next three years my grades dropped, and I was drinking more and more. I started to spend most of my time with friends that were doing the same thing. My sophomore year in high school I met Mike. I became pregnant and my mom threw me out. She had always told me that if I came home pregnant then I would have to leave. She stuck to her word. Mike's mom was a Christian and this is when I first found out about Jesus. In order for Mike and me to live under the same roof our lives needed to line up with the word of God so my mom agreed to me getting married and signed the papers. I was seventeen, married with one child. At eighteen I was married with two children and using meth.

For the next ten years Mike and I stayed married. Our whole marriage we used Meth and drank consistently. Our marriage was full of lies, deceit, and abuse; verbal and physical. Neither one of us were faithful from day one. In the midst of this we were raising babies and at the same time trying to become grownups ourselves. In 1999 we were divorced.

The next few years I was with a man who became the father of my fourth child. I was clean off of drugs for the first year but slowly began using again until my addiction destroyed our relationship. After this relationship, my life went into a complete spiral downward.

In 2003 I was involved with a man who started off as my drug dealer and shortly after became the father of my fifth child. This relationship was extremely abusive. I became isolated that year from my family and pretty much the rest of the world.

When I was six months pregnant the police came and raided our motel room. We had been committing numerous crimes to support our addiction and someone told on us. I remember to this day the relief I felt when I was put into the back of that police car.

My son's father went to prison for four years and I was released right before I gave birth. I spent the next year in a Christian rehab where many seeds were deposited in my life. I completed the program and stayed clean for about three years afterward.

In 2006 I was buying a house with my mother, going to church and working. Life seemed to be better than before but there were still demons lying in wait. I was saved but I wasn't completely set free. During this year my youngest daughter ran away, my son became incarcerated and my oldest daughter became pregnant with my first grandchild.

I was still very much connected to the people who I was close to in the streets and when things became completely overwhelming, I went back to the neighborhood and by the end of that first night I was high again. I didn't know yet the true POWER of God. The POWER that is able to deliver and withstand!

In 2009 my home that I lived in with my daughter, youngest son and two grandchildren was raided for maintaining a residence for gang activity. My daughter was living with me while my son-in-law was gone on deployment. She and I went to jail and my son and grandchildren were taken by CPS.

By this time, I was smoking PCP regularly along with using and selling meth. I was involved in things in the streets that weren't safe for me or for my children for that matter. I look back now at God's hand over us.

They brought my son-in-law home to release my grandchildren to him and eventually my daughter was cleared of the charges. I remained in jail and my son went into a temporary foster home until his now adoptive mother (my ex sister-in-law) received custody of him. From this point on my life only spun more and more out of control. Even losing my son to the system wasn't powerful enough to break the chains that had me in bondage.

The next few years I spent in and out of rehab and then eventually back in the streets. The courts were awarding permanent guardianship to my son's now adoptive parents and I was so far into the lifestyle of the streets and my addiction that all I could find the strength to do was stay numb. Meth had become my means of support and PCP my means of escape.

Through a tragedy in 2012 something began to shift inside of me and God started gathering all the broken pieces of my life. I had left for Texas in February with my daughter and grandchildren. The police had been looking for me and I was so far gone in my head that days would go by and I wouldn't even notice. My daughter told me she wasn't leaving without me and she didn't. That twenty-four hour drive I slept the whole way.

When we arrived in Texas, my mind felt separate from my body. That is the only way I can describe how the drugs left me feeling. I hadn't used in twenty-four hours for the first time in a long time but I couldn't feel back to normal.

I remember being so scared that I was going to be lost in my own head forever. I know that doesn't make sense but if you know anything about PCP you know that the high is something completely evil. It separates your mind from your being, almost like being out of the body. The state I was in felt as though I just couldn't return to myself. My daughter, grandchildren and I were in a motel waiting for her military housing to go through. That night I told my granddaughter to lay on the bed with me while I read her the Bible. I can't remember what I read but the next morning I woke up with my mind clear.

For the next four months I stayed in Texas. I was clean and in shape taking care of my grandbabies and even had a job babysitting. The beginning of June, I received a phone call telling me that one of my very best friends was shot and killed. This is the tragedy that affected the shifting in my spirit.

In the streets there were things I stood for and ideas that I valued and held to be true. These very ideas now had taken the life of someone I loved very much. In that world of addiction, destruction and chaos we had these false ideas of loyalty, respect and rules to abide by. I say false because it was all a lie of the enemy to keep us in bondage.

I claimed to be so in control of my life, my surroundings and my day to day affairs but when I heard the news of my friends death, I knew at that moment just how out of control my life really was. I went back to Bakersfield a few weeks later and it wasn't the same. I just knew that I had to change my life. Of course, it wasn't that easy and it took another almost two years before it happened.

I was home for about two weeks when I got picked up by the police on my warrant. I got out a few weeks later but for the next year and a half I was continuously in and out. During this time my brother and sister-in-law lost their home and we all ended up on the streets; my brother, sister-in-law, their children and me.

We were committing crimes to survive and to feed our addictions. This period of time was worse than any before. My involvement in the streets along with my brothers was getting to a point where I could literally sense death around the corner. It was so dark that year and to this day when I look back it's as if a whole chunk of time just stood still.

July 2, 2014 God intervened and said enough was enough. I was in a motel room with some friends and the cops raided us. I was arrested for possession of counterfeit bills. When I went to jail all control was completely stripped from me. My brother was pretty caught up at the time and I had continuously felt this false sense of being able to protect him while I was out. In jail I couldn't do anything.

I was scared my brother was going to die and I was all out of answers. One night in my cell I so happened to not have a celly and I finally broke. I fell on my face screaming out to God to Supernaturally change me! I told Him I didn't just want to feel better for the moment, but I wanted Him to transform me. When I came up off the floor the weight that was lifted was unreal.

A couple days passed, and I received a book from the Chaplain titled, *Life Supernatural* by an author named Lynetta Dent. I began to dig into the Word of God like never before. When I tell you, "God was talking to me," he was talking to me!

August 31, 2014 through September 2, 2014, I along with two other girls fasted and prayed. I asked these two friends of mine who were also being transformed by God to come into agreement with me for my brother's life.

The first night of our fast God gave me the book of Esther (NIV) in the Bible. He told me that just as Esther was brought into position in order to save her family so was I. "For if you remain silent at this time, relief and deliverance for the Jews will arise from another place, but you and your father's family will perish. And who knows but that you have come to your royal position for such a time as this?" (Esther 4:14 NIV)

I knew that night as God spoke to me that if I didn't completely allow God full reign of my life that my brother would die and so would I eventually. I still to this day KNOW that I heard God loud and clear. The third day of the fast, September 2nd I had come out of prayer and asked God to give me a word. I opened my Bible and he gave me, "But we had to celebrate and be glad, because this brother of yours was dead and is alive again; he was lost and is found." (Luke 15:32 NIV)

From this point forward, I have had a relationship with Jesus Christ. The difference today is I know Him personally. He speaks to me and I to Him. There are so many promises He has given me that have come to pass and those that haven't, I know have already been taken care of in the spirit.

I am free from addiction and every other bondage that Satan tried to destroy my life with. No, things didn't happen completely overnight, but I stood on what God said. Deuteronomy 31:8 says, "The LORD himself goes before you and will be with you; he will never leave you nor forsake you. Do not be afraid; do not be discouraged." (NIV) He goes ahead in the spirit and completes what He promises. Today my brother and his wife are free from addiction and in ministry.

We all have a past that sometimes is dark and broken but I believe wholeheartedly that God will take that road and piece it all back together. Anything you may have been through does not have to be in vain. God will take it, build upon it and His Glory will shine.

All those broken pieces of my life from my childhood, to getting arrested that final time, God is using today. Not only am I free but He uses me through being a substance abuse counselor to speak Hope into the lives of others.

No matter what you may be facing, God has a plan and a purpose for your life. All it takes is to say, "I am all out of answers God, take over!"

DIVORCE

"ABOUT 40% TO 50% OF MARRIED COUPLES IN THE UNITED STATES DIVORCE, ACCORDING TO THE AMERICAN PSYCHOLOGICAL ASSOCIATION."

RETRIEVED FROM
HTTPS://WWW.APA.ORG/TOPICS/DIVORCE/

DOMESTIC VIOLENCE

THE ADVOCATES AT THE NATIONAL DOMESTIC VIOLENCE HOTLINE ARE AVAILABLE 24/7/365 TO TAKE YOUR CALLS AT 1-800-799-SAFE (7233). THEY ALSO OFFER LIVE CHAT SERVICES VIA WWW. THEHOTLINE.ORG 24/7/365.

3

THIS IS REALLY MY LIFE

Sharon Finney

This is really my life.

𝒯hese are the five words I constantly uttered over a ten-month period. As I slowly opened the envelope and began to read the words on my divorce decree, those five words were still in my mind and spilling off my lips. I learned a lot of "legalese" throughout the year of separation and ultimately, the divorce process. Now, it is all reduced to typewritten words on multiple pages, signed, sealed, and officially delivered to my temporary home. My legs weakened as they often do when I receive difficult news. The reality of being alone, with three very young children had become official. The ink was dry on the papers.

Even though I asked for this, the thought was unbearable. It was also a reality I tried to prepare for longer than I wanted to admit. Though it seemed inevitable, why did this have to be MY truth? Did this have to happen to us?

I grew up with both of my parents, two people who remained married until one passed away. Is it fair that my children would enter a place I had never been? Or live a potentially uncomfortable life I had not lived? How am I going to help them through the difficulties they may encounter?

Satisfactory answers were nowhere to be found, and I was tired of coming up with more questions. Oh, here's another one. Are they going to hate me for choosing this life for them?

My mind is constantly filled with thoughts and feelings; which, in turn lead to my countless stories. But I feel some semblance of confidence because I have made a comeback more often than not. As I share my adult life in various settings, I present my do-overs, failures, victories, and simply put, the lemonade from the life lemons I accumulated. One thing I know for certain is how merciful our heavenly Father is.

There was a time when I thought divorce was the absolute worst thing ever. I even shared in one heartfelt discussion that if I could survive divorce, I could survive anything. Now, I realize that while you're in a painful place, it can't help but to feel like nothing could be worse.

One minute, I'd try and resist beating myself up for getting divorced, while the next, I would search for the silver lining. This choice thrust me into the world of single parenting. On top of all of that, I have dealt with job/career changes for the sake of family. It seems there has always been something to deal with while hoping for a favorable outcome.

Divorce was not forced on me. This bold step was a choice; the result of my very own decision. When I felt in my mind that nobody was benefitting from the marriage, I FILED; but that did not make it any easier. It was HARD.

I reached a point in my life where I just didn't want to talk to anyone about my problems anymore. I was tired in more ways than one. Instead of talking, I started writing my feelings out. I learned during my darkest hours that holding things in literally ate away at me. I felt pain inside that could not be described in words. I even reached a point where tears would not fall. Sleep was undesirable because I was afraid of what dreams would come to me due to the deep thoughts overtaking me.

Twenty years later, I try not to lament on those past feelings. Yet, reminders are there. Things happen to bring it fully to the forefront of my very existence. What do I share with others considering this step? If both parties realize this is where it's going, or what you think you want, it can still be extremely difficult. I can't identify more than two divorced couples who said it was easy. When people choose to marry, vows are taken with intentions. Because we are not perfect, mistakes are made. Forgiveness is expected. Occasionally, feelings of resentment set in. This is reality for so many including me.

In a perfect world, everyone would just work through it and manage to stay together. But life has shown me through imperfections that the horrible "D" word, divorce, sometimes seems like the only way.

I have been blessed to celebrate remarriage and share that happiness with anyone who will listen. My husband and I have regained a sense of normalcy, but none of this was an overnight fix. It truly has been a process.

It's all starting to sound like a soap opera!

I never imagined being a single parent because of how my story came to be. I graduated from college and got married right away. After years of building a career, I started a family with my then husband. I really expected the relationship to last until death do us part; because, even though there were issues, we were still together. The intent and my expectations were to work through the challenges we faced. Unfortunately, many unresolved issues became justification for toxic behaviors.

The more I contemplated options, the less I felt it humanly possible to survive on my own with three kids. They were so close in age that life was always a balancing act. Somehow, God made a way. There was always an unexpected resource, a ram in the bush, that encouraged me to hold on a little longer. But the time would eventually come to pack up the little ones and figure out a plan without my usual problem solving.

My losses included money, time, material things, and more money. But thanks be to God, I maintained faith. Please don't think I never experienced doubt. I don't think I questioned God, but I suffered spiritually.

In fact, I sat in many church services where the words,

matter what. As I tried to convince myself that I would be single forever, I had a heart-to-heart talk with God. I had a keep it real, tell Daddy how you feel kind of moment.

I was tired and frustrated, so I cried out and said, "Lord, I have been doing this single parent thing for a long time. People say I am good at it, but that is not what I feel. If this is how it's going to be, you have to show me a better way." My heart was at peace after this prayer. I had not been that sincere in my prayers in a while. But God heard me. Then the most unexpected thing happened.

A friend happened to be visiting during hurricane season and became stranded in town beyond her intended departure date. We hunkered down with a family member for several days, which gave her time to fully observe where I was in my personal life. I was not aware of her actions, but because she knew about me, she took a very bold step.

Weeks later, once she returned home, she encouraged me to contact a guy. She and her husband were friends of his and seemed to know him well. He lived in another state, was around my age, and was also single due to divorce, just like me. I was not interested because I had already discussed with the Lord the help I needed as I continued down the path of single parenting. I really didn't care to hear what this friend had to say.

I came up with excuses as to why there was no follow through on my part; however, after a few messages asking if I contacted him yet, I gave in and sent an email. I would eventually learn that this gentleman was the father of three. We both were the parents of two sons and a daughter. We also learned of other similarities including prior military service, a love for music, and enjoying opportunities to travel.

After several email messages, we had our first phone call. Before I knew it, we were reading a 30-day study and having nightly phone discussions about it. This gave us time to get acquainted in a different way. I never had such an experience with anyone, so it was different, interesting, and fascinating. Once we completed the study, we decided to meet in person. The agreement was to remain friends even if we didn't feel right after the face-to-face interaction.

Much to our surprise, we felt completely comfortable enough to stay connected and see where the relationship would go. I believe getting to know each other over those weeks of studying together gave us a much-needed foundation. Our relationship was not love at first sight because we were many miles apart in the first eight weeks of learning about one another.

We managed to meet up in person again two more times before getting engaged. Now, please understand, we had only known each other about 90 days when he proposed. Two imperfect beings with a desire to love again had met and decided to give this relationship thing another try. After the engagement, we thought of marrying the following year. Conversations with trusted, God-fearing loved ones gave us the confidence to marry two months after getting engaged.

So again, the world went into shock with the news.

I look at my three young adults, reflect on my years as their mother, married, divorced, and remarried, and I must express gratitude. I must thank God for giving them to me, for trusting a broken vessel, the wretched (wo)man that I am to be their mother. Who am I, and to what do I owe this honor? I owe it all to God!

I love the Lord and I appreciate the many opportunities that He has granted me. I also thank God for another opportunity to be a wife. My open demonstrations of gratitude are not to brag, but to show that I recognize grace, as God blessed me with a husband to love me and be a father to my children. This man took on the duties and responsibilities of six children: three step and three biological.

When I reflect on my brokenness, it dates back to various phases of adulthood. Though a few pages in a book can't possibly capture or explain it all, I know how each affected me, and I am not blind to the fact that some stay in a broken state. Why was I not included in that group? I may never know but I will always be grateful! Therefore, no matter what is thrown in my face and no matter what I am reminded of, I will always give thanks.

I know what it means to feel too far gone to be worth saving. Yet, God spoke to my heart, leading me to a place of complete trust. I stopped worrying about what might be said, or how others might fill in the blanks of my story and I remembered that somebody would eventually be blessed by it. I will keep sharing how good God has been and continues to be to me for the one that needs it. I am nothing without Him. Stay blessed!

Many Blessings
Candy L. Moses

4

FROM ANXIETY BACK
TO PEACE

Candy L. Moses

I wasn't in love with him, but I had some sort of love for him. I convinced myself that I was lonely and needed someone in my life to love. I was feeling some type of anxiety. I acted in desperation and did not clearly think about my actions. God's word tells us to be careful, meaning anxious for nothing. *(Do not be anxious or worried about anything, but in everything [every circumstance and situation] by prayer and petition with thanksgiving, continue to make your [specific] requests known to God Philippians 4:6 [Holy Bible*

Amplified Version]). In hindsight I know I just settled for my ex-husband.

I had been friends with my ex-husband since we were nine (9) years old and I dated him in high school. We never really broke up, we just were apart. I couldn't afford to go to college, and I knew I needed a way to live outside the comforts of my family's home. I thought my ex-husband and I would be together; I just did not have that thoroughly planned out. So, upon graduation from high school I went into the U.S. Army.

My ex-husband was already working a job in high school so, when I left for basic training our path together diverged. My ex-husband lived his life, and I lived mine. We reunited at our 35-year class reunion. He told me that he had never married, and that I was the only woman he had ever wanted to marry. After many phone calls and plans to spend time together he asked me to marry him and I said yes.

Of course, there were warning signs, but I ignored them all because I had known him since we were kids. This loving, gentle-spirited young man I had known would never hurt me, and of course I would never hurt him. We had been friends for so long. I thought we genuinely cared for each other.

I thought that a 40 plus year friendship was a strong enough foundation to build upon. I knew I would be able to support his vision and life goals. I knew I would be happy together with him. I thought he would be happy with me too; however, I was extremely wrong!

My ex-husband and I married on February 14, 2014 (his choice). I thought that was so romantic, in addition to being an easy way for us to remember to celebrate our love and anniversary. I was diagnosed with breast cancer in May 2015. I started treatment in June 2015 and retired from my job in July 2015. Things quickly disintegrated from there. You see up to that point, I was the only one working and supporting us. I even paid for the entire wedding - my dress, his suit, the cake, reception, catering, even our rings. I paid for everything; allowing him to go to school for his master's degree. Cancer and retirement knocked the blinders off my eyes harshly and with a quickness. We separated June 5, 2016. I celebrated my Untethering Day (divorce) on June 27, 2018.

June 4, 2016, my ex-husband beat me up and strangled me until I fell unconscious. He went to jail that night/morning of the 5th and remained there for a little over 90 days. I went to the hospital with a busted lip and bruises around my face and neck. We never lived together again, but we continued to attend the same church once he got out of jail.

I am a very private person about my personal life, but at the same time I am an open book. I'm not going to lie about me if you ask me a question. I felt everyone at church knew what I had just been through, but I was not quite ready to put it out there. I refused to hide myself even though I felt humiliated and embarrassed.

You see, when my ex-husband and I joined the church we always sat together and matched our clothing colors as much as possible. We always arrived together in the same vehicle. He almost always had his arm around me when we were together.

Now we sat on opposite sides of the church and arrived separately. As a matter of fact he was living in a homeless shelter and rode the church van to and from church. I tried my best to avoid him. He tried his best every week to get in my face and introduce me to his new shelter buddies saying, "This is my wife...."

One Sunday he was even sitting in the front of the church with his arm around another woman who had ridden the van with him. So, everyone in church now knew for certain, if they hadn't known before, we were no longer together. Yes, it was difficult, but I refused to show it as much as I could. I kept my head up high in public, but I beat myself up and suffered through emotionally at home when I was alone. I was personally and emotionally devastated! I was in mourning.

I had support from my children, but I did not tell what my feelings were inside. How I truly felt inside was for me to bear alone. I could not express it out loud to anyone. I had already forgiven him for hurting me that same night. In fact, I didn't even want him to go to jail. I just wanted him **to get the hell out of my house** and never come back.

I was grieving the loss of a 40 plus year friendship. I was angry at myself for making such another huge mistake in my life by marrying him. I ignored all the warning signs not to do so. I disappointed my mother and children and exposed my grandchildren to someone I now wish I hadn't. I felt so stupid, ashamed and worthless. I felt that I failed God and myself yet again. I decided I needed to regain myself. I needed to be restored and healed so I could move on. I had to get those feelings, those emotions out so I decided to go on a fast.

My spiritual father called me and agreed with me on fasting. He told me to fast and pray about regaining my joy, my love, and my peace. He said that I had lost those elements of myself. I didn't really agree because I felt at peace somewhat. I loved everyone just the same. Joy was there I supposed.

My thoughts were that I just needed to get over the loss of a marriage and friendship. I put on that brave face in public, so all was well outside. But inside, at home..., I just knew I needed to feel better. I needed a release.

Even though I didn't necessarily agree about the peace, love, and joy, I obeyed. After all, this is my spiritual father. I have a history with this man as my father. He prays for me always and encourages me. He calls me when I least expect it and always has a word from the Lord for me. He also consoled me about the lies my ex-husband was telling on me about the marriage and final fight. He told me, "You can out live a lie."

I had never heard that before. My spiritual father explained to me that living right before God would be the truth I could stand upon. My life would speak for itself. **I can outlive a lie**.

I fasted and prayed. A huge part of my fasting and praying has always been journaling. I studied scriptures on peace, love, and joy. I journaled about what I read in those scriptures and how they applied to my life. I released my grief over the loss of the marriage, the loss of the longest friendship I ever had, the loss of all the finances I had invested, and the loss of all the time and love I invested in the relationship. I wrote out all my feelings. I wrote out all my emotions.

Tears often stained those pages, but I kept writing. What I couldn't say out loud I could say in writing and I did; however, I was not totally free yet. My biggest problem to acknowledge and overcome was forgiveness. This forgiveness was not for anyone else but for me.

Forgiving and releasing others was never a problem for me. It was and actually still is very easy for me to do. I know that people are not perfect. I know that even though people know better, they still make mistakes and bad decisions from time to time. My problem is forgiving myself.

Even though I am quick to say "no one is perfect, we all make mistakes," somehow, I fail to include myself in that sentiment. I hold higher expectations of myself.

I didn't cut myself any breaks. My little mess-ups were huge failures to me. I admitted all this to myself, owned it and also owned that I needed to make a serious change otherwise I would never regain my sincere love, joy, and peace. I would never stop putting on that brave face. That brave face would continue to just be a "brave face".

I begged God to help me. "How can I do this? What do I need to do? It's so easy to forgive others, but how do I forgive me? Why can't I just forgive me?!"

I heard God tell me as plainly as I could hear anyone else speaking to me: "**Who do you think you are, to not forgive yourself!?! I forgave you! Are you more than me? I created you! So, who are you not to forgive you?**" Wow! What a revelation! I so needed that! God had from the beginning forgiven me. (*Or like we say colloquially, God* **been** *done forgave me*).

Forgiveness is a choice. You make up your mind to forgive someone and you do it. You do it because of love. If you love God and have His heart, you love His creation, His people. John 3:16 says "For God so loved the world, that he gave his only begotten Son, that whosoever believeth in him should not perish, but have everlasting life." (Holy Bible, *King James Version*) I am a creation, a people of God.

I deserve to be loved and forgiven. Some of the love and forgiveness I am so willing to bestow on others, absolutely must also be bestowed upon myself. I must love me and forgive me as much as God loves and forgives me. I finally forgave me. I finally released myself to succeed and to fail. And it's all going to be okay. Peace and love washed over me, and I felt joy again.

I was no longer marching in place. The brave face finally vanished. I began moving forward again, but more importantly, I was really hearing from God again. Whatever was stopping up my ears and muting or muffling God's voice to me was completely gone. I could feel his presence and his guidance again. I was no longer doubting my ability to hear from him anymore. I could and still can see the door to my future open waiting for me to walk on through.   Whew!!! Take a deep breath…Ahhhhhhh!

Dear Father in Heaven, thank you for giving me strength and courage and also encouragement to write this portion of my experience, my journey. I am praying that whomever may need this will find it and be encouraged that they are not alone in this type of life struggle. I pray that they will read this and not go down the same path of desperation and anxiety that I travelled, or if they are in the midst of a similar journey that reading this will be a guiding light to the open door you have already prepared for them, be they woman or man. *Father, I am also praying that they find* YOU *in finding themselves, and that they will find themselves in finding* YOU. *In Jesus' name I give you praise, honor, glory and eternal Thanks. Amen.*

5

MOVE: GOD'S PLAN

Taylor Stephens

*A*llow me to introduce myself. My name is Taylor
Daniela Elyse Stephens, born Martha Jean Taylor.
I am a single mother of two teenagers and the survivor
of domestic violence. Yes, you are reading the words of
an educated woman with a history of being emotionally,
physically, financially and mentally abused.

It is my sincere desire that someone is encouraged, blessed
and revived with new hope after reading what God has
done for me. If nothing else, understand that what truly
matters is where God is taking you. I was several years
into my adult life when I grabbed hold of the realization

that no matter what it looks like God had never left me, forgotten, discarded me nor had He ever forsaken me!

I remember vividly going through my years of abuse at the hands of someone else. What I remember most is feeling disconnected, lost, forgotten, worthless and useless. Self-esteem was non-existent. It did not take long for me to begin to believe the things being spoken to me by my abuser.

For years I had been told that I wasn't as pretty as other women; that I was not smart; that I was not capable of doing anything outside of sitting at home; that nobody else would want me but him. Feeling defeated I believed that in some way I had earned the treatment I was getting. I even questioned God! WHY?

At my lowest point and when things became extremely horrific, I even became afraid of sunsets and sunrises. I was afraid because I did not know which day would be the day that my children would no longer have their mother. I had already been pushed down a flight of stairs, punched, bruised, left out in the cold barely clothed with a blanket (as punishment), knocked unconscious (waking up on a bathroom floor with my son rubbing my head crying) and doors kicked in on me.

No one truly knew the extent of what was happening with me because I did not want anyone to know. I learned to be an amazing keeper of secrets. Public perception was that he was nice, polite, handsome, smart, exceled at his profession and was a respected brother in our church. Who would believe that this man would ever be capable of committing such horrible acts against his wife?

What people need to understand is that unless you live behind a closed door with someone you will never really know who they are. Because I was so good at keeping THE secret, how would anyone know what happened to me if I ceased to be present? In my mind the best way was to write a letter and I remember the day that I sat down to write this "timeline". I did not address nor mail this letter out to anyone. I had just written my "if something happens to me" letter.

I know what it feels like to be afraid of someone you love. To love someone who treats you like a queen one day and an unworthy being the next. I know what it's like to believe that no matter what he does or says he really loves you. But I also know what it feels like to be afraid to leave.

I attempted to leave once. I wasn't able to get far before a Sheriff pulled me over, detained me and gave me these options; go back with the children or they go back without you. We all went back, and it was a long time before I even had the courage to think about leaving again. I knew after that failed attempt that I had to have a more fruitful plan.

How was I going to do this? I did not have a job (I had not worked in years). So how was I going to support my children? Where would we live? I prayed for months for an answer. I asked God to help me form a plan, to show me a way. I prayed that God would answer me; I desperately needed Him to give me a plan and give me a way. He knew our needs and what I desired.

After months of praying God showed up and He ANSWERED!

The Plan Enacted

It was a Friday morning and I was praying as I usually did but on this day, I kept having the word "move" run across my mind. There has never been a doubt in my mind that God took a complex situation and made a simple plan: "move"!

That entire day I kept having that word run through my mind. At this point in our marriage my ex-husband was in a military profession on a specialty assignment that took him away often. The same day I kept thinking "move" was the same day he was due to go away for the weekend on assignment.

God had given me a plan in one-word; "move"! That is what I had asked for, right? So, why should I panic? I didn't need to since I was faithful to Him; so, I listened, and I "moved"!

I "moved" with only the clothing, food and other basic essentials for my children that I could pool together. The plan was to "move". It was not first pack all your stuff, get the furniture and whatever you can get in the car then move. I had asked for something, He told me what to do and I was obedient.

I got into that car with nothing but the clothes on my back. I strapped my children in their car seats, said a traveling mercy prayer and headed towards healing with only enough money in my grasp for gas. I left, and I never looked back! That was ten years ago.

It was not easy being on my own. There was a sudden realization that I was now a single mother of two small children. I was a survivor, a broken woman in need of Gods repair. What I learned after God pulled me out of the trenches of my life was that: No matter what it looked like He had always been with me. He kept His promise! It took months for Him to move on my behalf. Later I circled back around to the understanding that I asked, and he answered in His time not mine!

Listen to me; no matter what it looks like, no matter what you are going through, no matter how isolated you feel, just know that God can turn any situation around. Don't believe me? Look at where I am today. I left an abusive relationship with just my children, the clothes on my back and a car.

The ALMIGHTY Provides in Our Obedience

Jehovah Jireh blessed me in abundance, more than double for my trouble. Less than two months after leaving, I did what seemed to have been impossible for someone with a lack of executive work history. I accepted a position with the Federal Government at the pay rate of GS-13.

While I was praying all those months, I was also doing my part by secretly applying for jobs because as we all know faith without work is DEAD! I entered the system at an executive level. It was that position that enabled me to earn the money that I would need to file for divorce, which I filed for five months after leaving.

I was able to provide for my children without fail and I was able to rebuild. Remember all those material things I left behind? I was able to replace all of it easily. Less than one year after leaving, and with the help of God, I purchased a home for us.

While in that position I was asked to perform an additional duty as the Directorates Suicide Prevention Trainer. That additional duty opened my eyes and my heart to the world of Social Work.

WOW! I am here to be an advocate and to support those who cannot fight for themselves. I am here to assist those who desire to be well holistically, and I became an advocate for leveling the playing field. An advocate for social justice! He took the weak and made her brave!

Masterpiece

Each person has it in them to be remarkable. God does not make trash, He does not create less than. You will hit some roadblocks and see many hardships in life but holding fast and staying connected to Him is the foundation for making it through any situation.

He took a minimally educated woman and allowed her to experience some of the worst that life had to offer and turned her into an educated, four degree holding woman who has a license to practice a medical profession. I came out bruised, but I recovered and you can too. He changed everything about me and allowed me to begin a new life. I am not saying it will be easy, but it is worth it; YOU are worth it!

God made everything about me new. The only original identifying piece of me is my date of birth. He allowed for things such as a name change. He worked through government systems to do what is difficult: obtaining a protective order and getting a new social security number under the federal guidelines for domestic violence to assist with safeguarding my personal information.

When He brought me out, He did everything He needed to do in order to ensure that his child was as safe as possible.

It took a long time, but I now walk with my head held high. I walk in my destiny! I walk confident in the work that God has done with me, within me and through me.

You may currently be sitting where I once was, or you may have recently "moved" from an abusive relationship.

I am here to tell you that you need to possess the strength to break up with all the negative parts of your life that are weighing you down. I broke up with sadness, depression, negative places, people, things, habits and thoughts. I held onto nothing that kept me confined to the prison that my marriage had become.

Moving Advice

When I moved on with my life, I was extremely careful with whom I interacted with. My advice to anyone exiting a difficult or abusive relationship is to get to know yourself before you graduate into another relationship. Yes, being alone is not something people desire. However, I came to quickly realize that being alone does not necessarily translate into being lonely.

Take time to rebuild and get to know "you". Make your way before you insert another person.

I chose to not be in a relationship the first two years after being divorced. I needed to learn who I was as an individual. I wanted to cement our smaller family and I needed to learn how to be the best single mother I could possibly be.

I craved to build myself up so that I would make better decisions when it came to relationships. I desired to fuel my self-esteem and have a firm belief in my self-worth so that I would never fall victim to another unhealthy relationship.

You will never be able to forget your trials, struggles, hurts and hardships but you can move past them. I admit that I never wanted to forget my past. This may sound odd but remembering where I came from helps me to ensure I do everything possible to never go back. I have "moved" on.

I have dated but I have yet to run into the partner that I believe was made for me. In speaking about dating, ladies and gentlemen, if you have children, they do not need to be introduced to every person that you decide to spend time with. Safeguard them, their emotions and stability because they look to you as the example and model of what relationships and intimate interactions should look like.

I challenge you to get to know yourself before you step into a committed relationship. I also challenge you to get to know any person you plan to be with prior to making a cemented commitment. Learn about them, their family, their history, and do not be afraid to ask questions. I'm not suggesting being paranoid; however, I am suggesting you learn enough to understand what motivates that person.

What patterns, family history (pathology) assisted in creating the person you're interested in? Learn about love languages. Yes, love has many languages and if you don't communicate love in the same manner then think about whether you really want to settle for someone who communicates love in an alternate manner than you do.

So, I will graduate to this: stop thinking that you can change another person. Stop thinking that you are the problem and if you change it will get better. Those are all the thoughts I had.

Individuals have the absolute power to change themselves, but they have to want to change. You will never be able to live the dream of being the savior and changing your abuser's behavior. Ultimately, I understood that my situation was going to get worse and likely not better, so I "moved" towards a change in living and circumstances.

If you are on the outside looking in and know someone who is in an abusive relationship do not be judgmental. It is easy to give advice when you are not the one living in pain. The most common advice and statement communicated by many is "why don't you just leave?" I cannot tell you how many times I've heard that. Try to be that person's peace. Do your best to be a part of the solution and attribute positively to the process. Give hope because when you are in the midst of an abusive relationship hope is at a deficit.

If you are in an abusive relationship there are a multitude of resources available for you. One of the resources I used during my planning to exit was the drafting of a safety plan. This became a blueprint for me to use when I found myself flustered.

No safety plan is going to be the same. A safety plan should be personalized. It should include safety methods both in the relationship and when you are planning to leave as well as after you exit. I included within my plan how I would communicate my situation to the people that were closest to me. I also addressed what legal action I planned to take once I had reached my destination after exiting.

Make use of whatever assistive resource you can grab hold of. Be Well!

Email: taylordestephensmove@gmail.com

SICKNESS

AND

MENTAL ILLNESS

**OUR ATTITUDE AND BELIEF
SYSTEM GREATLY AFFECT OUR
OUTCOME IN SICKNESS AND
MENTAL ILLNESS.**

**WE ARE REMINDED IN ISAIAH
53:5** *BUT HE WAS PIERCED FOR OUR
REBELLION, CRUSHED FOR OUR SINS.
HE WAS BEATEN SO WE COULD BE
WHOLE. HE WAS WHIPPED SO WE
COULD BE HEALED. (NLT)*

**SO...WHOSE REPORT WILL YOU
BELIEVE?**

6

GRACE TO RECOVER FROM SICKNESS

Novice McDaniel

As I was pondering and reflecting on the goodness of God, I began to thank Him for the many storms that I have endured in my life. There were some storms that He delivered me out of. He snatched me out of the fire and out of the hand of the enemy. On the other hand, there were some storms that God delivered me from. I never saw the storms; I never even knew that there was danger on the horizon or in the forecast. Then, there were the storms that God delivered me through. I had to endure the entire storm. Through it all, I came to know the God that I once only believed in.

At some point I came to the realization that my faith in Jesus is stronger because of my experiences with Him. A few years ago, I went through an ordeal with my health. If left to the plots, ploys, and plans of the enemy, I would be either dead or seriously challenged in my mind and body.

As the result of two Transient Ischemic Attacks (TIA's), or minor strokes, I was diagnosed with a congenital heart defect. This defect is called Patent Foramen Ovale (PFO). In laymen terms, I had a hole in my heart. This hole is found in the wall of the left and right atria of every human fetus. Within a few months after birth, the hole closes for most people. In my case, the hole did not close. It caused blood to leak from the right atrium to the left.

It did not pose a problem until the leaking blood contained blood clots. According to an article published by the American Heart Association, the human body produces blood clots all the time, but the lungs will filter them out. In my case, the blood clots passed through the hole in my heart and moved to my brain.

I thank God for Jesus because when I was diagnosed, it was discovered that I had an area on my brain that revealed the existence of a prior, untreated, minor stroke. But God! I underwent heart surgery to close the hole that was in my heart. I continue to give praise to the Lord because even

65

though there was a hole in my natural heart that needed to be closed, I did not fear because God had already closed the gap and occupied the hole in my spiritual heart. He lives and dwells on the inside of me, by faith, in the person of the Holy Spirit. My heart was fixed because my hope and my trust were in the Lord.

I am not exhorting myself to be this great woman of faith and power. I had faith in God, but fear came. Yet, because of faith, fear went. I surrounded myself with people of faith. My husband kept me lifted up before the Lord and he allowed the Lord to minister to me and love me through him. I read, and I listened to the word of God and I filled my home with praises and worship unto God. I cried to God many days and nights.

When I look back at this period in my life, I realize that through the sickness, the doctors' visits, the medications, the sleepless nights, and the weakness, I had an encounter with the true and the living God. I did not have any doubt that God would heal me. Once I received the report of the physicians, I went to church and my pastor gave me the report of the Lord!

He told me that the sickness was not unto death and that the Lord was going to multiply my years. I took those life-changing words, confessed them and held on to them. The conviction of my heart and the confession of my mouth were and remains that whether by life or by death that God would be glorified in my body.

I remembered the year prior my pastor preached a message that changed my life. In this message, he talked about Shadrach, Meshach, and Abednego. These three Hebrew boys were thrown into a fiery furnace because they would not bow down and worship a false God. I was not going to worship this illness and I was not going to let it be the topic of my every conversation.

The young men made three confessions before being thrown into the fire. They acknowledged that God was well able to deliver them from the fiery furnace. They believed and confessed that they knew God was going to deliver them. Moreover, they declared that in case God did not do it, that He is still God. They believed that the Lord would honor their prayers, but if not, He is still God!

Allow me to clarify the statement, "But if not." It is not a statement of doubt, fear, and unbelief. Rather, this statement confirms the Lordship of Jesus Christ in our lives. It lets the world know that God is sovereign, He has the preeminence, and that we trust His way over our own needs and desires.

You see, I realized something. I realized that God would either heal me to remain on the earth for His purpose or He would grant me the ultimate healing of entering into eternity to forever be with the Lord. I was prepared for both. If you are a child of God, you do not have to fear death because absent from the body, we go to be with the Lord.

In other words, we must fight the good fight of faith in every situation, every storm, and in every battle. In my experiences with the Lord, I have learned that regardless to the conditions, our position is that we win every battle, all the time! We win! Hallelujah!

You can handle whatever sickness and diagnosis you receive from the doctor as you continue and end your lives with Jesus Christ. He is our beginning, our ending, and everything in between. Sickness and death are subjects that most people would rather leave unspoken; however, they are inevitable to all human beings. Our acceptance and ability to cope with these difficult issues becomes a matter of perspective and a matter of our faith in God.

Realize that God is sovereign, and He is always a loving, caring, and sharing heavenly Father. Even when issues seem to prove otherwise, God always has our best interest at heart. He is always good to us independent of the circumstances and the issues of life. When issues and storms arise, I encourage you to exchange the desire to fight, and the urge to fear for the opportunity to pray. In other words, get God involved in your circumstances.

I encourage you to have faith in God who is within you and

above you and He will enable you to handle the people, problems, pain, panics, and pressures that come against you and happen to you. You can handle every issue that you face because the greater One lives on the inside of you and He gives you the power to do all things. Always remember that the grace of God is sufficient for your life. His strength is made perfect in your weakness.

Endure hardness as a good soldier of Jesus Christ, allowing patience to have her perfect work in and through you. Hard times, sickness, and the occasion of death will come: and, they are designed by Satan to make you hard of heart. These are not times to lose faith in God. They are opportunities to draw closer and learn more about your great God. Continue to stand on the promises of God and declare His word in every situation, remembering that your confession is your possession and you will have what you say!

Never give up and never lose your hope but train your heart to believe that things will always get better. Learn to hear the voice of God and hearken to the Spirit of God. Allow the ministry of the Holy Spirit to comfort, console, and encourage you to always move up and forward in the direction of God for your lives. Never leave God out of the equation and learn to always deliberately default to God in every situation. Lean on Jesus and have confidence in Him in all things and at all times.

Enquire of the Lord and dwell in His presence in the midst of the panics, pain, and pressures of life. Commit your lives totally to Jesus and give the devil no place to influence or depress you. Draw closer to God daily and He will draw closer to you.

Satan desires to have you that he may sift you as wheat and as a person that is weak in faith. He comes to steal, kill, and destroy. He wants to steal your faith in God, kill your hope because of God, and destroy your life in the face of God. He wants to torment your life and then kill you. I pray for you that your faith in God will not fail. Let the confessions of your mouth and the belief of your heart resound and demonstrate that your Redeemer lives, and that God will be glorified in your body in life and in death.

In my walk with God, I have learned that worship, praise, and giving of thanks are always the proper responses to whatever situation that I face. In my worship, I began to acknowledge that God is my loving, caring, and sharing Heavenly Father. During my time of challenge with sickness I began to acknowledge the Lord as Jehovah Rapha, the Lord who heals. Some people say that healing is not for us today, but I know that the Bible is true and that the Lord is our healer. Whether by creation, miracle, or by medicine, it is the Lord who heals us and takes sickness and disease out of the midst of us. Exodus 23:25

(KJV), *"And ye shall serve the Lord your God, and he shall bless thy bread and thy water; and I will take sickness from the midst of thee."*

He is Jehovah Shammah, the Lord who is always present with us. God is always at hand and near to us. He is always available and willing to help and heal us. We simply need to trust and depend on His ability and willingness to help and to heal us. In Deuteronomy 31:6 (KJV), we are encouraged with these words, *"Be strong and of good courage, fear not, nor be afraid of them: for the Lord thy God, he it is that doth go with thee; he will not fail thee, nor forsake thee."*

In my worship, I acknowledge the Lord as Elohim, the God of creation, restoration, and new beginnings. He will heal us, and He will restore us. He will make all things new in our lives because He is El Roi, the God who sees, knows, and cares about everything that concerns us. He looks upon our sicknesses, hurts, heartaches, disappointments, and pain with the intention of working things out in our favor.

If you are experiencing sickness for yourself or another, remember that God is a very present help at all times. Allow the Lord to minister love, peace, blessing, and healing into your situation. Remember that there is nothing too hard for God and He will deliver you from all of your enemies, including illness if you call on Him and allow Him to. Always remember that God's healing is complete, and He will begin to heal you with His peace and change you in the midst of your storm even before the storm is over.

When you find yourself in the midst of a storm, be mindful not to suppress emotions that need to be expressed. Doing so can lead to depression. God gave us emotions and they serve needed purposes. Our emotions serve as outlets and safety valves because we have an innate need to respond to given situations. The Bible speaks of occasions when even Jesus wept, encouraging our hearts to know that God cares for us and He cries with us.

I thank God for turning His heart towards you and for stretching forth His hand to heal you from the crown of your head to the souls of your feet. Because of His loving kindness, I declare that you will walk in good health all the days of your life. I pray that the Lord will teach you to number your days and to apply your heart unto wisdom. Please realize that the same Spirit that raised Jesus from the dead now lives in you and because of that, your mortal body is alive and functions properly according to God's Divine protocol and design.

7

THE ELEPHANT IN THE ROOM: THE TOPIC THAT'S OFTEN AVOIDED, BUT ABSOLUTELY NECESSARY TO DISCUSS

Dr Monica Debro

*M*any people are dealing with the badgering thoughts of suicide. This methodology of controlling life's situations has become more rampant over the past few years. People are losing hope and giving up on life. They are giving up on their future, their dreams, their goals, their families, and their hopes that things will get better. Suicide is not prejudice. Satan's attacks of suicidal thoughts do not have a preference on which it affects. Rich. Poor. Famous. Infamous. Not known. Affluent. Leader. Follower. High on the hill. Low in the valley. Extrovert. Introvert. Christian. Non-Christian. Healthy. Sick. Young. Old. All races and nationalities. Thoughts of suicide and fulfilling those thoughts are affecting people all over the world. According to CDC Principal Deputy Director Anne Schuchat, M.D. "Suicide is a leading cause of death for Americans – and it's a tragedy for families and communities across the country."

Is it the inner me or the enemy?

For as he thinks in his heart, so is he. Proverbs 23:7 NKJV

What are you thinking in your heart? What are you saying about yourself every day? Could what you're saying about yourself or the concern you have for what others are saying about you be the root of the thoughts to cause self-harm?

Where did these thoughts originate from?

I will share with you where the negative berating thoughts originated from for me: in junior high school. At some time during junior high school, I started thinking that I wasn't good enough, pretty enough, curvy enough, didn't dress "hip" enough. I mean, I was so small that I was still buying clothes from the junior section.

Although I was on the cheer squad, track team, and basketball teams, I still dealt with the inner pangs of low self-esteem. Standing on the outside looking in, people didn't realize that I just didn't feel as though I was enough. I had the book smarts, but desperately wanted to fit in with the "cool crowd." In my opinion, it never happened. You know how peer pressure can be, wanting to belong to a specific group in the school.

I thought things would finally change during my sophomore year. I was participating at a Baptist state convention and it was being held in our town. My father was a pastor, so we were always at the summer Baptist State Convention no matter what city it was being hosted. Well, this one year, I had learned a poem by Dr. William Herbert Brewster titled "I'm Determined to Be Somebody, Someday." The poem had six (6) stanzas and I learned every word in preparation for the convention.

There were other students participating from various cities. I was very nervous and felt every emotion as I looked into the faces of a standing room only congregation of people from around the state. I energetically recited this poem. I didn't just recite the poem, I had movement and webs and flows of voice inflection as well.

When I finished the poem, I received a standing ovation and to this day, I remember some of the faces of my classmates yelling great job and class of '89. At that moment, I took a deep breath, a sigh of relief, and thought "they finally see me. I'm finally somebody." Little did I know that long before that night, I was already somebody and just needed to believe in myself.

Well, the accolades lasted only a short time and I was back to feeling the low sense of identity and low self-worth. Now, nobody could tell this from the outside because I appeared to be a happy teenager. In actuality, I was hurting inside.

My senior year, I was driving home from church with my mother in the car. As I parked the car on the pebble rock driveway, the tears began to flood down my face. Those uninvited and unexpected tears erupted an onslaught of pinned up emotions, thoughts, and feelings that I'd been having for months. You see, the devil had planted a mustard size seed of a false imagination in my mind that I would not see graduation; that I would be dead before our graduation date.

Those were scary thoughts for a teenage girl to experience. I don't remember anyone committing suicide growing up. Yes, we had several classmates die in drowning accidents, but suicide, not that I can recall. Having these thoughts frightened me and I didn't know what to do about them.

As I put the car in park and my mother realized I was crying, she looked at me and asked what was wrong.

When I told her, she responded in her loving country tone "that's the devil and he don't know what he talking about. You won't die before graduation. You will live." From that moment, she guided me as only a mother could with prayer, love, gentleness, patience, and comfort.

Many women and men are holding on to a label that was placed on them as an adolescent, teenager, college student, or as an adult. Our actions are motivated by our thoughts. When we wake up in the morning, we need to be intentional about thinking good thoughts. If we wake up thinking, "today is going to be a bad day," we've already set the stage for our expectations. Nobody told us it was going to be a bad day; it came from our inner thoughts.

How is it that we wake up sometimes with dread thinking it's not going to be a good day? How do we have this thought when we haven't even sat up on the side of the bed and put our feet on the ground? Those thoughts are attacks of the enemy.

When I wake up in the morning, the first thing I say is "hello Father." I acknowledge Him because I know he's been watching over me and is ready to hear my voice speak to Him early in the morning. Additionally, I am a firm believer in Proverbs 18:21 (NIV) which states, "The tongue has the power of life and death, and those who love it will eat its fruit."

Let's consider some action steps when we find ourselves in the crux of negative thoughts, specifically thoughts of suicide.

Action Step #1

The light shines in the darkness, and the darkness has not overcome it. **John 1:5 NIV**

Pray, seek God, and begin to fill your atmosphere with praise and worship music. The darkness of Satan cannot remain in a place where the Light is shining. When you invite the Light, God, into your environment, He will have dominion over the darkness, Satan. Your first action step is to overthrow your environment with God's presence. You will see and feel an internal change.

Action Step #2

Therefore, confess your sins to each other and pray for each other so that you may be healed. The prayer of a righteous person is powerful and effective. **James 5:16 NIV**

Although this scripture states to "confess your sins", I also see it as: confess your concerns, heartaches, pains, etc. to each other. With this in mind, we need to be open to discussing our feelings with family members, friends, coworkers, church members, etc. who may be dealing with thoughts of depression, low self-worth, and suicide. I encourage you to have open and transparent conversations about suicide and ask the question that nobody wants to ask, "are you thinking of harming yourself?" Shame prevents others from wanting to come forward, but you never know when the one-person God places along your path will be the person who needed someone to reach out to him/her.

I was at prayer one night and God said to me "ask her if she is thinking of harming herself." My initial thought was who? When I opened my eyes, they fell on a woman that I did not know. I'd never seen this woman before and didn't know her name. A flood of emotions washed over me, and I thought, "what if I really didn't hear God say this to me? What if this woman thinks I'm crazy?"

Then I began to think, "what if she is thinking of harming herself and I'm disobedient to what God has told me to do?" Needless to say, I didn't want to brush off the Father's words. The feeling was too strong, and I'd prayed for God to direct my steps. We have to be careful of asking God for something and not doing what He tells us to do. We have to trust His process and trust His plan. He aligned me to be a helper to those who are hurting and suffering in silence.

As we finished the time of prayer and I noticed that she was walking back to her seat to gather her things, I continued to pray and ask God for specifics of the words he wanted me to say. In His ultimate way, He simply responded, "ask her if she is thinking of harming herself."

I was standing beside her for a few seconds before saying anything. I stood silently praying for her and asking God to allow her to be transparent. When she looked up, I could see hurt and pain in her face. The tears were flowing from her eyes and she quickly tried to dry them. I touched her hand and guided her to sit down beside me. I introduced myself and in obedience, I asked the question I'd been sent to ask, "are you thinking of harming yourself."

Her response was a resounding "yes" while she nodded her head up and down with a new flood of unexpected and uninvited tears. At that moment, she couldn't speak any other words because she was emotionally and mentally tired and needed to have a release of the tears she'd been holding on to as a way of protecting herself. I held her in my arms and allowed her to feel the emotions that were pinned up on the inside.

God saved her life that night because she'd prayed for Him to send someone to speak to her. She needed to know that God hadn't forgotten about her and would always love, protect, guide, comfort, and heal her through the pain, discouragement, loneliness, and overwhelming sense of doom she was feeling.

My obedience in doing what God instructed me to do provided her a reminder to: Be strong and courageous. Do not be afraid or terrified because of them, for the Lord your God goes with you; he will never leave you nor forsake you. Deuteronomy 31:6 NIV

Now, some may think we should've had a conversation before leading into my question. I'm not a beat around the bush type of woman and to me this would've been delayed obedience. God didn't send me to her to have "fluff" conversation before addressing the necessary. He sent me to her for a specific reason.

God   is   within   her,   she   will   not   fall;
God   will   help   her   at   break   of   day.
Psalm 46:5 NIV

Whatever it is that you're going through, don't you dare give up, don't you dare give in. This might sound cliché, but things will get better. Whatever it is that has you wanting to end your life, it will soon dissipate. Whoever it is that has hurt you to the point of thinking your life isn't going to change or that things won't get better, soon, they won't have a hold on you.

You may have been told something negative related to your:

- ❖ Appearance

- ❖ Family

- ❖ Friends

81

- ❖ Finances

- ❖ Home

- ❖ Ability to succeed

- ❖ Personality

Some of the words that may have been said to cause harm include: "You're not:

- ❖ Good enough

- ❖ Beautiful

- ❖ Strong

- ❖ Smart

- ❖ Loving

- ❖ Courageous

- ❖ Financially stable

- ❖ Assertive

- ❖ Supportive"

I don't want you to attach these negative words to who you are by allowing them to have a harsh influence on you. Prove the person speaking negativity to you wrong! Prove the situation wrong! Show it, them, and yourself that you are stronger than any obstacle, person, place or thing that has attempted to weaken you to the point of wanting to end your life. Your life is worth living! #Love2Life

Action Step #3

"Do not let any unwholesome talk come out of your mouths, but only what is helpful for building others up according to their needs, that it may benefit those who listen." **Ephesians 4:29 NIV**

In my version of this scripture, I transform it to "Do not let any unwholesome talk come out of **my** mouth, but only what is helpful for building **myself** up according to **God's** needs, that it may benefit **me/others when I hear the words being spoken**."

I've learned to transition God's Word to meet me personally where I need it the most. There are many times that I change a word to my name to make it more personal. With this scripture, we should remember that regardless of what others say to or about us—we are commanded to speak what is good.

Action Step #4

I have hidden your word in my heart that I might not sin against you. **Psalm 119:11** NIV

Whenever a negative thought comes to you, immediately replace it with a positive affirmation or scripture. I encourage you to find some scriptures to refute the thoughts that Satan places within your mind. I've had to make scripture cards during the times when Satan was attacking my mind. Yes, I have God's Word hidden in my heart, but there were times when Satan was choking my thoughts and I needed these scripture cards to fervently focus on scriptures that would speak to me as I read them aloud.

Because God has full authority of our future, we will not give up, we will not give in, we will not allow the thoughts of suicide to have control over us because God's plans are perfect and true, we plead Jeremiah 29:11 over our future!

> For I know the plans I have for you,
> declares the Lord,
> plans for welfare and not for evil,
> to give you a future and a hope.
> Jeremiah 29:11 (NIV)

My prayer is that with this writing, you are able to look within, see, and value your worth. I pray that you will gain additional wisdom of how much God loves and cherishes you. I pray that you will find an accountability partner, support person that you can confide in regarding your feelings. I pray that you are open to listen without judgment to someone who will confide in you. I pray that you will be assertive in speaking positive words consistently until you begin to believe in the power within to live without fear and in full confidence of who you are but more importantly Whose you are; a daughter of the King.

References:

Center for Disease Control and Prevention (2018). Retrieved from https://www.cdc.gov/media/releases/2018/p0607-suicide-prevention.html

8

COPING WITH AND OVERCOMING DEATH AND ANXIETY

Roxanne Robinson

The day came when I thought it was time to meet my maker. Within a short amount of time, multiple tragedies engulfed my life. I became weak, my heart began to palpitate, breathing became slow, and I felt lightheaded. In a panic all I could think of is to yell for my children to call 911. As I stood up to run their way, my leg gave out and I fainted. Although my children were around me, their panicked voices seemed so distant. One was screaming call 911, and the other saying it will be okay: the youngest crying, while the oldest trying to console him. The ambulance took me away.

While in the emergency room they ran many tests, the diagnosis was a panic attack and dehydration. An IV of electrolytes and a restart of my anxiety meds was what the doctor prescribed. I had experienced these symptoms multiple times prior, minus the fainting. The physiological effect had taken over my body; consequently, my thoughts and fears had overwhelmed me.

Where It Began

Early on I began to experience anxiety attacks, unknowingly. At the age of seven or eight, my mother would repeatedly leave me home alone at night. She would wait until I had fallen asleep to leave, so awakening in the middle of the night not being able to find my mother was scary and that left me in a state of worry. Constant crying and tremoring were what I did until I was able to fall back asleep. This was behavior that lasted for a couple of years and it taught me how to live in fear and worry.

These feelings resurfaced after I lost someone very near and dear to me, my little cousin. We grew up like siblings because our mothers were close sisters. When our mothers were out, we were always at grandma's house. My cousin had great love and admiration for me. He never called me cousin, but "sister". I worried about him a lot when he was a teenager, growing up in the streets of Detroit. Any unusual call, worry would creep in and that lay dormant inside me.

When he was approaching 30, I began to feel much better because he made some impressive life changes and was on the right path. To my amazement, my cousin finally decided to move to North Carolina with my children and me. They had the greatest love for him, he was fun and joyous, a big kid at heart and my children loved having him around. I was happy to have family in North Carolina now. After settling in our home, he had to return to Detroit for personal business reasons and would return within two weeks for my daughter's high school graduation, they were so close.

Unexpectedly, I got the call about a week after he left. On my way to second service at church, I had an immediate breakdown while driving. The death was a tragedy: sudden and unforeseen. This was the first time I experienced such a reaction. At the wrong place, at the wrong time, he was murdered, execution style. I was numb for two days.

When this tragedy occurred, I was managing hotels. I could barely function at work but somehow pushed through, by the grace of GOD. Many days I would go into an empty room and cry and cry. I would go home and shut myself off from the world and cry even more.

My job was already a stressful job, managing multiple hotels and one particular location that produced high levels of stress. I was living in distress. During my grieving time, overworked and overwhelmed, there was yet another tragedy. One of my hotel managers called and told me there had been a murder at my other property. When I arrived, I learned that the hotel guest was shot in the head just as my cousin had been.

I was still grieving my cousin's death so needless to say, the stress increased, and the panics became more frequent. Because of my dedication to the job, I continued to work but it became unbearable. I requested a job transfer out of the property level, but it was denied. The stress and anxiety became so unbearable that after a couple more months of working, I had a nervous breakdown. My doctor took me off work for three months.

During this time is when regular counseling sessions began, and I was prescribed long-term medicine to improve my health. At the time, I did not have much of a support system; therefore, I had to endure this alone. I attribute this to why my healing took longer.

At one point during my episodes, I was in and out of the hospital so frequently, I was withering away and praying for my early death. I had no strength to go on. One panicked call from my daughter to their father was enough for my ex-husband to contact my uncle (God rest his soul), to come to North Carolina and look after me.

My uncle was a natural caregiver to his family, so he came and stayed for nearly two weeks, which was a blessing from God. It gave me the willpower to feel again. He took care of my household domestically and made sure my children were taken care of. When I took him to the bus station, it was the first time I experienced separation anxiety disorder. Panic arose again.

I was in counseling to deal with my anxiety. The counselor referred me to a psychiatrist and I worked with an awesome psychiatrist. When I began seeing her, I did not want to live anymore. I felt guilty for living while my cousin was not living. My family had a high death ratio and I had been to many funerals of very close loved ones. I had already lost my parents, my grandparents and even a child so when my cousin passed away it sent me over the edge. I came to the realization that part of this anxiety came about due to the loss of my father being murdered in the same manner. I wanted to die too.

At the time, I did not realize the effects it would have on my children if I were to depart this earth. I was caught up in that headspace. I just wanted the pain to stop and that was the truth of the matter.

I had become obsessed, googled every symptom, self-diagnosed myself and concluded that I was dying. The self-diagnosis didn't sit too well with my primary care physician. I can tell she felt as if I was losing my mind; therefore, she recommended I go see a therapist, but I was already in therapy. Ultimately, I ended up off work for this condition for an additional two years.

Coming Out of The Shadows

One day a spirit came over me and I realized there was more to life to live for. I realized that I could overcome this, and I would find a way to succeed. I was inspired to try and give it my all. My children were afraid and helpless, and I was their mother, their protector and provider. I owed it to them, if not myself, to live and be healthy. They were being neglected.

I knew the power and strength within me. I no longer accepted that I was helpless and could only rise above with the help of a support system. I noticed when I changed my perspective and my focus, I could feel victory growing inside of me.

When you have a sense of determination from an internal self-motivation, mountains can be moved. I began to remember what brought me through a very tough childhood. In high school, I noticed a quote on the wall that read, "Where there's a will, there's a way".

I took that simple quote and applied it in life and navigated through with that mentality. It took me many places and elevated me in areas I could not believe or imagine. During this time, I also came across a very popular poem called, Don't Quit. I recited that poem and memorized it and said it aloud many days in my teenage life. Again, I used this to get me through.

I had the tools in my back pocket all along; I had to pull them out. Once I was able to decide where I wanted to go, the plan came for me to get there. It was time for me to come out of the shadows and live again, for my children and myself. We all have the strength and capability to pull ourselves through. Sometimes we look for others to save us and we have the tools inside.

My psychiatrist could immediately see the change in me and expressed her observation with amazement and admiration. She asked what I had been doing because she saw a change in my energy, my attitude and my expressions. I told her that I decided I wanted something different and remembered what I was capable of and my worth and value.

I reminded her of the many obstacles and trauma I overcame before, independently and silently. I ended by saying, "plus I am determined not to have dependency on the anxiety meds and that it was time to wean me off of the medicine".

I shocked her with my boldness. I told her that I wanted to

be a speaker on the topic of dealing with and coping with anxiety. I wanted to inject life back into people suffering with anxiety. Before anxiety meds were mass produced, people were experiencing the same symptoms and trauma and somehow made it through without medication and I had confidence that I would be one of those individuals.

She was so impressed and supported my idea, offered support and encouragement, and told me the value I would bring sharing my experience and techniques I used to assure and encourage others. She assured me that she had the utmost confidence that I would succeed, considering how broken I was in the beginning. It felt like a miracle and I wanted to share it.

We gradually weaned me off the medicine and some days were tough, but my determination was tougher. She was impressed at how I managed through the transition and maintained my attitude and growth. I am forever grateful to have had her as part of my recovery process.

Stepping Into Healing

I was determined to find a way to overcome my situation without having the support I so desperately needed. I figured there are many people in this world that have overcome many tragedies and I was going to be one and share my story. I was introduced to holistic options to contribute to my healing.

My first step was yoga, recommended to me by a dear friend I met when I first moved to NC and she and her family welcomed my family into her home. Shortly after, she moved back to California. I was speaking with her one day, from many days of crying out, and she recommended yoga. I was not familiar with yoga but was willing to try anything to heal. I began to search for yoga studios in my small-town area and found one.

This was the beginning of my journey to recovery. This instructor I call a masterpiece because he transformed me. My body was getting much needed exercise from being curled up in my bed and on my couch as I suffered.

It was refreshing and was in the morning, so I was able to take in the brisk weather. The portion that was most effective for me was the last five minutes of meditation and speaking life into us. I felt my soul open up. He was speaking life into me. I felt the difference it made and decided I wanted to speak life into others coping with anxiety.

For a long time, I worried about dying or my children. It nearly drove me insane. I was panicking, and checking on them throughout the night, worried when they left the house. I spoke with a few women of the church who redirected my attention to God and focus on loving them and making every moment worthwhile, rather than making myself ill. I could not control or predict the future. That put it into perspective for me.

I have many people to attribute my healing to, many in passing, one or two encounters and every little bit contributed. I embraced it, every small act of kindness. It changed how I dealt with and treated people. We do not know what someone is going through or growing through and any small act of kindness can attribute/contribute to one's healing.

I had to make some lifestyle changes that would help my healing in order to regain a quality of life. Some of the practices that helped me tremendously were reading my daily devotional to feed my spirit, yoga, bi-weekly massages to release toxins from my body, weekly acupuncture, therapy, and getting out around people. Often times I had to go alone, and it was hard. I had to remind myself of the purpose and mentally push myself. Going out and being in the land of the living and absorbing the positive energy, slowly crept into my spirit. I began to feel the change. To have some engagement, I sought out people with genuine, caring hearts to sit with and express my concerns and fears. They encouraged me and uplifted me.

Everyone experiences fear and anxiety in some form through circumstances. A Deaconess at the church attributed my anxiety to my realization that I was mortal, and I affirmed it. When the anxiety becomes debilitating is when help should be sought.

With generalized anxiety there is persistent, uncontrollable and irrational thoughts of worry, which leads to physiological experiences. That could be heart palpitations, headaches, exhaustion, lightheadedness, aches and pain. The mind causes serious duress on the body. I began to experience these symptoms in my body. Once I took care of my mind, my physical body began to heal.

We cannot escape anxiety or death, but the key is self-care and mindset management. Being mindful and consciously present in the moment helps control your thoughts from focusing on the past or future. It brings a better quality of life. Be around positive people and find hobbies to enjoy and set a determination to overcome. Have faith in God and faith in yourself. I have faith in others that they can rise above their circumstances and be the light and motivation for others, as I desire to be.

Everyone experiences fear and anxiety in some form or fashion and it is circumstantial. Whatever the situation, whether through death, trauma, combat, assault: you are capable of making it through.

SINGLE PARENTHOOD/ TEEN PREGNANCY

Life is not over unless you stop fighting so put on your spiritual gloves and fight like the winner you are!

~Shirley D. LaTour

9

LABOR IS NOT EASY

Sandi Johnson

*A*s little children, we enjoyed fairy tales and using our imagination to create our ideal world. Our thinking, dreams, and goals were limitless. As we ran on the playground, skipped rope and shot hoops there were no boundaries on us.

We were free to dream.

It was something that many times as teenagers we screamed, "I cannot wait to be grown" while frustrated with the rules that were imposed on our freedom.

As teenagers, while trying to find ourselves, there was still a belief that the world was all ours. Jumping to the college years, we learned of the evils of the world but still had lust and amusement for life with the promise of our dreams becoming reality. Then one day we looked up and this thing called adulthood was before us.

As true adulthood hit with all the responsibility, we forget that five (5) year old on the playground who believed that they could fly. As all the "adulting" causes us to lose sight of the childhood dreams, they are no longer on the forefront of our mind but pushed to the back of our thoughts. We may begin to ask, "How do you live your dream when life has become a nightmare?"

There was a television show some years ago where the host, Ashton Kutcher, would play practical jokes on people. They would set up a situation where the victim was left standing there looking shocked and in disbelief of the staged situation. At that point, Ashton would jump out and let them know that they were being "punked." In other words, this was not a real situation but a joke. At times in life, I have been waiting for him to jump out to tell me that I am simply being "punked" and this is not real life.

Life is moving fast, and events of life are occurring. These life events are not all positive or good. There are more financial obligations than financial resources with a daily to-do list that exceeds the 24 hours allotted in a day. We are trying to balance church, marriage, career, relationships, and children. The children come with a complete set of more items to fit on an already full to-do list like sports, dance, homework, recitals and the list goes on. One day we looked up and wondered again "how do you live your dream when life has become a nightmare?"

What I found to be the answer is that those nightmare moments are where the fortitude and skills required for your purpose path are being developed. It is in the midst of the midnight that we are becoming whom we were purposed and designed to become.

Many times as a single parent, I experienced those midnight times; and, as I reflect back, I now know that all the stress, pain, disappointments, and closed doors were for the good of the world. The skills it took me to stay the course as a single parent are the exact same skill set that has been required to launch a business.

I was truly a single parent, not a co-parent: there is a difference. I did not receive regular financial support and he lived out of state so there were no weekend breaks. I can recall one time I was short on money and our lights were turned off, so we played a game I made up called Darkness. In this game, we laid in my darkroom real close and told stories. My children loved the quiet, peaceful family time. There was no noise, not even the buzz of the refrigerator, and we were able to connect.

You may have never had your lights turned off in the natural but there have been situations that have come along that have tried to dim your light. It is when others are trying to diminish you, blow out your light, that we must stay connected to our Father and seek out the peace found only in Him.

Through the struggles of life, the repossession, foreclosure and divorce, we have all experienced some type of struggles although they may take a different form. Can you think of a struggle you have experienced?

It was during these struggles that I had to maintain a futurist mindset. This mindset focused on what is to come while embracing the moment along with the lessons. I had to look ahead because sometimes the present was just too hard. When I look back along my purpose path, I realize all the lessons are now someone else's breakthrough. All my hurts, failures, and disappointments are a springboard to healing for someone.

The financial shortfalls forced me to create other income streams that increased my computer skills. I would make invitations, programs, bookmarks, and custom candy bars. The skills I acquired at my most difficult times are essential for my company, EnVision Your Life. The futurist mindset always has the thought of "where I am today is not reflective of my tomorrow".

At one point, I was living with my two young daughters on

Turner Street in Detroit, MI. This area was a high crime, low-income area with the majority of my neighbors receiving some type of government assistance. I believe that I was one of the only persons on my block that went to work daily. There was one woman that would speak on her way to her office on the corner, where she was the product. My mind focused on raising my children to be productive, successful human beings and I refused to allow this temporary situation to determine the future, their future.

Those little babies with those six little eyes looking at me and depending on me for everything grew up. They just did not grow up okay, but they grew up great!

My daughters will be graduating from college in May 2019 from the same university. The university did not have a two for one special on tuition, but we were on God's plan. Both held leadership positions on campus including Student Government President and Public Relations Chair. Remember, I had to have side jobs to assist financially.

Another side hustle was coordinating events and my children were the setup crew; yes, child labor. Sydney, my oldest, was an instrumental member of the Campus Activities Board, which organizes events on campus; so, being the only kid in third grade that could put a seat cover on and tie a bow paid off. I have proclaimed that I BIRTH GREATNESS and so do you.

For my youngest, the baby boy, college the first go around was not successful and he has taken a different path than I envisioned. His purpose path is his own to decide and mistakes will be made along the journey. He has discovered a passion for photography. I still birth greatness and so do you!

Even if those kids are not going according to plan, you still have to claim it and speak it. Some of you may not be parents; and, after talking to others with children, may not even desire it. You still birth greatness. You know, those dreams that you had as a child on the playground, the goal you had as a teenager to be grown and never be like your parents or that vision and passion deep inside you that you had in college is greatness that only you can birth.

Those things that are trying to come forth, but fear is trying to halt it: that is greatness. Proclaim it that you birth greatness.

That notepad with ideas that you are even afraid to share with your spouse or friends is greatness. That book that you have been procrastinating on writing is greatness and ONLY you can birth it. That career jump you want to take is greatness. That business you want to start is greatness. I proclaim that those with children have birthed greatness in the natural and for all your visions, your dreams are greatness.

As parents, at times that greatness you naturally birth will have you late to work or appointments. You will be up late when they are sick. Many cities have designated places like fire stations to be safe drop off places for unwanted babies. Your greatness with feet will have you wondering if there is an age limit for dropping them off. Just like your children will make you late at times, your vision will keep you up late at night or will not allow you to sleep late in the morning. Most of my ideas come to me at four (4) am and God refuses to change that set creative idea appointment time.

Bringing your dream into reality will not be convenient or within your comfort zone. It may cause you to struggle and sacrifice financially to bring it forth. You have to remember that you birth greatness even when it does not look like it. You have to proclaim it, speak it, believe it and walk in it. "I birth greatness." Anything that comes out my body and my mind is greatness. The hard parts experienced along the purpose path are just equipping you for the tasks to come. It is building your skills and developing the character needed for the final destination.

You have to remember that you birth greatness even when your children decide to have a spaghetti fight and your house looks as if a spaghetti bomb exploded. Case in point: I had coordinated a bridal shower on Saturday and was exhausted. All I wanted was a nap, a few hours of rest. After church, I picked up my nephew, who was about 10, to watch them so I could nap. I had a lot of leftover spaghetti from the bridal shower, so I fed them and went to nap.

When I woke up, still feeling tired, I stumbled into the kitchen and had entered the spaghetti war zone. There were noodles, sauce, ground beef, bell pepper and cheese all over the stove, floor, counters, and walls. Cold spaghetti in the kitchen led down the basement stairs and all over the basement. Spaghetti covered my children: my greatness.

As I snatched off tomato sauce filled clothes and threw them in the bathtub, tired and exhausted, I built endurance and grit. I was exhausted, but I had to put my house back together. I had to scrub that sauce and grease off the walls, floor, and stairs.

As I cleaned up the war zone, I learned that no matter how bad the situation may look, with hard work and a plan it can be rectified. Now I know that when I hit snags in business, with a plan and grit, it can be overcome.

How many of you have had a spaghetti fight moment? A time when you were simply tired and exhausted, but something happened so pressing that it had to be remedied at that moment?

I could not leave those noodles, tomato sauce and ground beef all over my house just like you cannot leave your book unfinished, that business not launched, your event in the notebook, your new career not started, or your children not raised. It has to be taken care of now and only you can birth it.

Birthing Your Dreams

How do you begin to birth this dream, your dream? Remember I said you have to keep your vision in the forefront. The vision for my children was for them to be independent productive members of society. That vision was on the forefront.

One way I started keeping my vision on the forefront was by doing vision boards. I created a vision board, not a reality board. Have you taken the time today to dream? Have you taken the take to remember those childhood dreams, teenage goals or young adult aspirations? When was the last time you truly reflected on your purpose and clearly set a goal? Not an idea but a goal with a deadline.

After I started doing vision boards, I found out that they worked. My first one worked so well it scared me and I quit for some years out of that fear. The images that I simply glued to a white piece of poster board manifested themselves.

I found it to be such a powerful tool for establishing a clear vision that what started as a girlfriend afternoon has been birthed into a business. Your gift, passion, and hobby are your business; so, if you are looking to start the process to birthing the greatness in you, make a vision board.

The other thing that I did to birth greatness was getting some midwives to help the process. In the natural, you have a team that helps bring forth life. In the delivery room, there is a team of doctors, nurses, coach and maybe even a doula to help facilitate the process. It is the same with your vision and dream.

You need individuals trained in the birthing aspect of your vision. I have developed midwives by attending events such as seminars and conferences. At these events, you not only obtain knowledge, but you connect to likeminded people: the people who will midwife your vision such as Business, Life and Accountability Coaches.

I attended a conference in May 2018 where I connected with three women who are my support system, resources, and accountability partners. Do you have people in your life that are holding you to your purpose, passion, and vision? Well, seek them out by attending networking events, conference and workshops.

In conclusion, as you move about your purpose journey you will experience some moments of sleepless nights and days of "spaghetti fight moments." These experiences and "spaghetti fight moments" are just equipping you for the destination ahead.

Learn the lessons and maintain a futurist mindset while remembering that the current situation is not your final destination. While traveling along the purpose journey, take time to establish a vision board and build your midwife team by attending events with likeminded individuals.

10

THE BEGINNING OF TASHA

Shonda Curb

What if I told you that you could live through "IT"? Would you believe me? Whatever your "IT" is, it does NOT have to be the end. Life has a way of making you feel trapped and hopeless.

I know it looks impossible now. You made some choices that put you in an untenable situation, but it's not over. You're not finished! I believe you can do it, one step at a time.

I want to share a story; it feels like a lifetime ago. I had to learn to live through it too. And I did, in The Beginning of Tasha.

"The Beginning of Tasha"

God help me, I am 16 and pregnant. This morning, I went from having a scholarship to being a stereotype. I knew that Mother and the good "Reverend", or "Dad", would be angry. They were so concerned with "What will everyone think?" that they had long ago stopped caring how I felt. This is all their fault anyway. Let me tell you about it.

When I turned 13, I learned I was a "reconciliation baby". My parents' marriage had always been rough. They fell in love in high school but were too young to get married, so their love affair just created more affairs. Either the good "Reverend" or Mother cheated first; either way, there was a lot of fighting and "reconciling".

Mother never wanted children either, so imagine her surprise when a few months after a fight, she was pregnant with me. This is how they managed to stay together despite the struggle. As far back as I remember, they argued. By age10, I was praying for a divorce.

Last year, my prayer was answered. Mother and the "Reverend" broke the news, and my sister and I had the "privilege" of choosing who we wanted to live with. Some privilege! I was sure they already discussed which choice we would make. My only fear was losing my sister, Michelle. She would choose Mother because she let Michelle get away with anything, and I would choose the "Reverend".

I didn't choose Mother because I knew she secretly hated me. Why else would she give my sister the world and give me all the hell? I got all the responsibility and punishment, while Michelle got to coast, getting her way and acting like a brat. I know most older sisters probably feel the same, but I promise my mother really let her get away with everything. I couldn't go anywhere without Michelle. If she got in trouble, I got punished for it too. How does that work? I did all of our chores, because she had basketball practice. Mother called it "being responsible", but I called it favoritism. Even the "Reverend" and Aunt Vee tried to talk to her about it.

In high school, I finally got an opportunity to be normal. This is when I met Emma and Keith, the baby's father. Emma knew the loneliness I felt within my family. Her father was gone, and her mother was always working two jobs. When Emma started dating Johnny, Keith's cousin, she convinced me that it would be "safer" if I came too. I think she was scared because Johnny brought Keith with him everywhere, so they could cover for each other.

I wasn't interested in Keith sexually, although Emma encouraged us. Honestly, I was curious about sex, and he was willing to teach me. We were always careful to use protection because I didn't want to come home with anything that I didn't leave with, as the "Reverend" used to say. I was on birth control too.

Still, I knew the day I got pregnant. The condom broke, and Keith looked at me scared, as if to say, "What now?" I didn't respond; I just hunched my shoulders in an "oh well" manner. I didn't know what to say or do. It was too late at that point and I knew I would regret it. So, this morning when I realized I was late, I didn't think twice about purchasing a pregnancy test. I went to the pharmacy and called my best friend Kat. Kat would know what to do.

She looked at the test as I paced the bedroom. It didn't take long for her whole body to tense up and I knew the results without looking. The tension in the air was thick, it was crackling around us. "So, what are you gonna do?", she asked, worried. I wanted to cry, scream, run away.... anything to relieve the anger I felt towards myself.

Instead, I squared my shoulders, looked at Kat, surer of this decision than anything else I had ever done, and said "I guess you're gonna be an Auntie now". I had no plan, but I knew I could raise this baby right! I had been raising Michelle for a long time, and I was good with babies. Yes, it would change everything, but it was not impossible.

Keith's response

I called Keith and his only question was: "So, what are you telling me for?" As if, somehow, I got pregnant without him. I explained I was keeping the baby and heard him quickly say he wasn't involved; and, I was on my own. I know all he heard was "TRAP", but I really just wanted my baby to have a father.

I wasn't surprised that he was already backing out. That's how it is in the movies, too; girl gets pregnant, boy leaves, and girl has to figure it out alone. I wasn't expecting anything from him, and I was actually relieved that he didn't want to help. I could make my own choices. I didn't have to worry about trying to "make a family", I could do what I thought best with no objections.

I went to my aunt's house for some encouragement. She might not have liked to hear about the baby, but she would hear me all the way out. Oh, and give some tough love too. I tried to act nonchalant.

"Hey, Auntie, you busy? I need to talk."

"About what? You being pregnant?", she said it so candidly, not missing a beat.

How? I knew she talked to God, but He wouldn't tell her, would He?

"Yes ma'am," I said, bursting into tears. "How will I tell my parents?"

She gave me a huge hug. I needed it too because next, she let me have it.

"Now baby, you did this so now you have to live with it. Life is choice driven, baby. You made yours so deal with the consequences. What do you want to do?"

"Auntie, I did not mean to get pregnant! But I want to keep my baby!"

She looked at me over top of her bifocals and said, "Well, did you mean to have sex? Or did you slip and fall onto the man?"

"Well, if you look at it like that, then I guess so."

"She said, Sharell Baby, you've been looking for someone to love you back, for a long time. You did all you could to get it, and now you've got it. It's gonna be a tough road baby, but it's not the end. Just know that I'm here and I'm praying."

The Reverend's Response

I dreaded telling the "Reverend". He doesn't preach anymore, but he still has this "holier than thou" attitude. In his mind, I committed the ultimate sin. There's no way that I could have prepared myself for his reaction. When I came home, he was cooking. I thought it might be a good time to tell him because he loved cooking. I don't know how the conversation went, all I remember is being knocked out of my chair.

The last time he got this angry, he had his hands around my throat, and my head kept hitting the floor as he yelled and choked me. He isn't generally abusive; it was only the last couple of years that I've seen him like this. Like the time he "accidentally" punched me in the mouth. To be fair, I was getting between him and Mother during an argument. Now, I don't think the hit was meant for me, but my lips didn't know the difference and they started swelling anyway.

As he slammed me against the wall, he started talking about forcing us to marry. Keith didn't want to be a dad, so I knew being a husband was out. Besides, who was marriage going to fool? I was already pregnant, and most people can do simple math. I told him I wasn't marrying Keith. He told me he wasn't helping me, and I couldn't stay at his house.

His next statement made me lose all respect for him.

He told me I could stay, if I had an abortion. Some preacher! I was too angry to be confused at the hypocrisy. I knew I couldn't stay there. I did not say anything, but he couldn't handle what he saw in my eyes. I would never forgive him. He stomped off, probably to report to my grandparents what a disgrace I was. "Well, that went well", I thought, not even bothering to check for cuts or bruises. Since the nightmare already started, I might as well go to sleep.

Mother's Response

When I woke up, "The Reverend" was gone; maybe he was too ashamed of me. I drove to Mother's numb. After the encounter with "The Reverend", how bad could it be? I really didn't expect her to respond with anything other than name calling, or an "I told you so".

My favorite cousin, Randall aka Dirk, was there when I pulled up. I wasn't ready to face him, but I knew he had my back. I steeled my nerves and said a small prayer before going upstairs. Dirk was in the kitchen, eating as always.

"What's up ugly?", he said in our standard greeting.

"You are, stoner." I said, punching him.

"Hey girl, shut up. You breaking code." he laughed, pushing me back. Dirk was more like the brother I never asked for. We grew up together, literally. Our families even lived together a few times.

"I gotta tell you something, Dirk."

"What, dummy? Spit it out. What did you do dumb?" laughing at me.

"Shut up boy! I'm serious. Mother is gonna be pissed, but I can't wait because I already told Aunt Vee."

"Oh hell girl. You told one of them already, you know the whole family gonna know soon. What happened? You need a whooping anyway, you been too grown lately", he said it joking, but he knew I wasn't playing. I had broken code by telling an adult. We always handled things amongst the cousins first.

"If I tell you, you cannot tell your brother, you know he don't act right." Dirk quickly got serious. He was putting the cousin stare down on me when Mother and Michelle walked in.

116

"Tell what? You ain't got no business to tell!" Michelle said.

Well, here goes.

"Mother, can you sit down? I need to talk to you."

"Mother? Oh, you still mad, huh? I don't want to talk about this anymore Sharell." she said, immediately defensive. We had been having a disagreement for the longest about Michelle. I told her that Michelle was hanging with the wrong crowd, and she denied it. I told her that she was intentionally ignoring Michelle's behavior, and Michelle was taking advantage because of the divorce. After that, "Mother" is what I had taken to calling her, mostly because she hated it; but we both knew that I was right about Michelle.

"No, it's something else. I'm sorry...I made a mistake. I'm pregnant."

"How the hell you get pregnant? You still need somebody to change your diaper girl! Who is it, Tate or Cutter?" Dirk said, as he named everyone he didn't approve of. He always looked at us as his baby sisters.

"Dirk, please don't trip, you don't know him. But don't worry about it, he's not available."

Mother asked me what I intended to do, and I told her what happened with the Reverend. I also told her that I wasn't having an abortion or getting married. Then, she played her hand.

"If you give the baby up for adoption, you can stay here. But, I'm just not ready to raise a baby, Sharell." I thought I was going to scream, when Dirk interrupts.

"Hold up Auntie. Adoption? That's rough! You gonna make her go through the whole nine months and then give the baby up? Would you be able to do it?" I hadn't counted on Dirk to make a case for me.

"What do you want me to do Randall? I can't do this! And she knows nothing about being a mom. She's just a baby herself! What about school, what about money?"

This was my "IT". At 16, I had minimal support, a fresh pregnancy and no plan. I thought I would ruin both of our lives, but I knew Tasha needed me to try. That was 20 years ago.

Today, Tasha is 20, goes to college, and is on the Dean's List! I won't lie and tell you that every day was easy. There were some hard times...but hard times come and go to everyone just the same. I have no formula for you, or a method to help. There's no special way to get through it, and it does not have to be a pretty solution.

Just put one foot in front of the other and keep on walking it out. Just try it. You'll be surprised who you can become if you don't give up. Give your "best you" an opportunity to be molded by your adversity!

11

BROKEN, BUT I'M HEALED...

Truenice Bryant-Shaw

*H*aving been fractured, or damaged and no longer in one piece or in working order, having given up all hope is to be BROKEN. To correct or put right, to repair, to restore to soundness, and to restore to purity is to be HEALED.

Experiencing hurt is a universal experience; and, hurt can be caused by family, words, your own expectations, friends, people in the church, and the list goes on. It is a part of life, growth, and your purpose. We cannot avoid it and we will experience it in some way, form, or fashion. When we are hurt, we can carry the stench of lies, betrayal and pain with us. It can haunt us, follow us, and hold us back. But what if we were able to shed our suffering? What if we didn't allow our hurt to hold us back?

Well that was a woman about seven years ago, a twenty-two-year-old mother with one on the way. She was broken and in a very dark place...she was lost. You see, she had grown up in church all her life, participating in all the youth programs and singing and dancing, but deep down inside she was still this broken child.

She realized at the age of nine that there was something different about her, so she always kept things bottle up and stayed to herself, which allowed the enemy to put in her mind that nobody cared or understood her. The spirits of rejection, abandonment, low self-esteem and the needs to be accepted were the rulers of her life. She just wanted people to "like her." At the age of thirteen, she would experience her first heartbreak and built up a wall...her parents divorced.

That particular day, she knew something was wrong because her dad came to the school to pick her and her siblings up to walk them home, and as they got closer to the house, she noticed glass and things thrown in the street in front of the house. She and her siblings walked in the house and were told to sit down at the table because her father had something to say.

121

Watching her mother cry uncontrollably with her head down, she heard the words "I'm leaving your mom." She watched her mother cry day in and day out and one morning her mother came in her older brothers' room, laid her life insurance policies on his dresser and told him to look out for his brother and sisters. Suicide made its first visit to the home.

Her mother took off driving and she didn't know where she was going; they had just moved to Killeen. This little girl and her sister called and called their mom's phone but there was no answer.

On the third call they were able to get through to their mother, crying and screaming they begged their mother not to do anything stupid and proclaimed they needed her. Their mother had made her way all the way to the Still House Bridge getting ready to drive right off into the water. Her mother was hurt, and she was broken.

From that day forward this little girl began to watch her mother, how she would handle situations, how she would pray, how she would exercise her faith to get God to move on her behalf, but this little girl also began to look for the void that was left within from the abandonment of her father.

She was the true definition of a daddy's girl; and, although her mother put her in counseling to help, she ended up pregnant with her first child at the age of fourteen, a freshman in high school.

She was able to hide her pregnancy from everyone for six (6) months, matter of fact she tried everything she could to cause herself to have a miscarriage to get rid of the baby. That is a story all in itself. The only thing she could think of was the embarrassment it would bring her mom who was now an evangelist in the church and you all know how church people are.

Two Years Later

She is now sixteen, has given her life to God, and has gotten filled with the Holy Ghost with the evidence of speaking in tongues. She'd stood before the church and spoke her first message of encouragement entitled "Soldiers don't leave wounded soldiers on the battle field." She understood she had been chosen, but she did not understand what it would cost her to walk in her calling and the persecution she would begin to suffer.

It was in April of 2010 when she would experience her second heartbreak that felt like the ultimate betrayal from a sister in the church. The mistake that we make as god-beings is thinking that because a person professes Christ, goes to church, and knows all the church antics, and how to act like they walk on the clouds with Jesus daily, they are perfect. Yes, we would think they would know better, but that is in a perfect world. This is why it is so important to discern whom you allow to get close to you when you are in a low place. The enemy knows exactly when to assign what to your life to try to knock you off course. She thought she was just helping this sister in the church, not knowing the actions of this sister allowing the enemy to operate through her however, would knock her to what seemed the lowest place of her life.

She was raised up in the church, saw what her mother went through, was saved and filled with the Holy Ghost at 16, and she had faith that God could do anything but fail; however, she also began to question God, why? The bible says before we were in our mother's womb, He knew us, in Jeremiah 1:5. So He knew her, he knew the route she would take, the decisions she would make, but he also knew the strength she would begin to draw from the betrayal.

Even knowing this, she still could not understand why God would allow such a thing to occur that would eventually push her from the church for a period of time.

She turned her back and walked away, she gave away all her church clothes, put her bible on the shelf and began to rebel, living a life contrary to what she believed. She turned to the world, the very thing she hated, to fill the void that had been created.

As she began to live her life this way, anger, bitterness, hatred, and unforgiveness became the rulers of her life.

The enemy has a way of deceiving us and making us believe that his way is better, and he will even present a package that looks so beautiful and intriguing on the outside; however, inside the package are all the things that will put you on a path to destruction that will eventually lead to death. She was reminded of the hurt she experienced when her father abandoned her at thirteen years old and she felt her only option was to run from it. She partied, she drank, she engaged in activity that she knew with everything in her was against His will.

This is why it matters how you heal from the different experiences in life: it is important to forgive and not hold grudges because if and when you don't allow healing to take place, the thing that you thought was healed will heal improperly and eventually show its ugly face again.

By the time hurtful situations happen, and it is not dealt with properly or not at all and you grow, become wiser and get more successful, the hurt did not leave: it just concealed itself in your personality, perspectives, views, relationship approaches, policies, etc. A lot of people are allowing their hurt to dictate if they are going to continue life, complete their goals, and live in the abundance of life that God had given to them.

We make the mistake of listening more to the hurt than wisdom, instruction, and guidance. If we are not careful, hurt will have us doing all kinds of crazy things, but most of all, hurt will have us protecting a person that is not genuine or authentic. We have learned and will spend all our energy trying to camouflage and cover up or we'll build walls to prevent the most fragile and exposed places of our hearts from being easily accessible.

In this way, we end up becoming who God never ordained for us to be, which then causes us to take on a perspective, a view of classifying all people to be and do the same.

This was she, when asked, "are you okay" her response was always "yea I'm good." But really, she was a torn woman on the inside in a mental battle that didn't have any self-esteem or self-worth and some days she did not know whether she was coming or going. Things had gotten so bad that the same spirit of suicide that visited her mother when she was thirteen visited her.

With two toddlers and a newborn child, she was ready to just end it all, ready to be done with life because she figured no one would care anyway.

With her children in the bedroom, she went into the bathroom and locked the door. Tears streaming down her face, she grabbed the bottle of pills and began to throw her head back to wash them down with water. As she threw her head back, she heard the whisper of her heavenly Father's voice say to her "I have come that you might have life and have it more abundantly."

The doorbell rang. Through the door she heard the voices of her now aunt Jennifer Mackin and her First Lady (mother-in-law) questioning, "Where is your daughter, we need to get to her, where is she?"

As they were calling for her, she opened the bathroom door and began to walk towards the room door. She opened the room door and they grabbed her and began to call out the spirit of suicide. As they embraced her the tears still streaming down her face, they told her to sing... they said, "the song that is in your belly sing it."

She hesitated for a moment because she knew who she was called to be but at that moment she wasn't ready to surrender; She was ready to leave this world. She did not want them praying for her. She did not want to sing. She did not want to do any of the things they were asking of her but continue to wallow in her pity party.

But the more they prayed the more she began to break, and she began to sing, "to worship you I live." From that day forward, she made a vow to the Lord that she would never let anyone or what they did to her get her out of position or cause her to turn her back on Him because she didn't feel she had any value.

I was this hurt woman. I had to understand that hurt has been given a significant seat in the lives of the believer, but we have to refuse to live our life being led by hurt. In Luke 17:1 KJV Jesus said to His disciples "It is impossible but that offences will come: but woe unto him, through whom they come!" And so, we should expect them, we should prepare ourselves, and if you think about it, hurt has benefits.

Hurt is a part of life, leadership, ministry, and relationships. God leaves hurt for our development and growth. He wants us to be healed from the hurt because the thing that was hurt needs to be used by Him. James 1:5, It can't be wisdom if there is still pain.

So how do we move past the hurt, the offense, and the pain?

To stop loving isn't an option. Author Henri Nouwen writes, "When those you love deeply reject you, leave you, or die, your heart will be broken. But that should not hold you back from loving deeply. The pain that comes from deep love makes your love ever more fruitful." Unfortunately, pain is no stranger to any of us, though it is something we all desperately wish we could avoid. People have become so immune to hurt that they think it is normal and have accepted it as a way of life.

Dysfunction is comfortable, and some people don't always

want to be healed because of the excuse to be able to remain broken or fractured: they use their hurt to justify irresponsible, carnal, and ungodly behavior. Healing does not mean the damage never existed, it means the damage no longer controls your life.

But how do we get beyond the pain? Why is it so hard to just let go and start our journey to healing?

In my experience, I did not want to let go because I wanted the people that hurt me to hurt and suffer like I did. But I learned we must go through it and while going through it, take the challenge to grow through it. I realize the most difficult task for a person with a broken heart is to stand still and feel the crack but that is exactly what I had to do.

Because no shortcut is without its share of obstructions, you have to grieve in order to move on. By going through the intense pain, you eventually surface as a stronger person ready to tackle problems head on. Soon the pain will lose its stronghold over you because in reality that is all it is, a stronghold.

Strongholds are an incorrect thinking pattern that has molded itself into our way of thinking. These strongholds have the capability to affect our feelings, how we respond to various situations in life, and they play a large role in our spiritual freedom. We must renew our way of thinking.

Laugh and cry when you need to: laughter heals on many

levels. Monitor how you're going to heal, because hurt will always present you with an opportunity. When you experience hurt and respond to it the right way, it will add dimensions to your character, resilience, insight, and your love capacity.

Think about your life story, life journey, how have you handled hurtful experiences? Have you allowed it to create more fear or a greater level of righteousness? God can help you when you're hurt. Psalm 147:3 says He heals the broken hearted and binds up their wounds. I encourage you to Cast all your cares on Him, because He cares for you (1 Peter 5:7).

ABOUT THE AUTHORS

Visionary Author

SHIRLEY D. LATOUR

SHIRLEY D LATOUR is a native of Ft Wayne, IN currently residing in Killeen, TX. Retired Army Nurse Corps Officer, she is a Transformational Speaker, International Best-Selling Author and Minister of the Gospel. She is a Co-Author in two anthologies and has stepped out to offer others a voice in writing through her own publishing company, SL Elite Publishing. She has been featured on such radio shows as KRGN 98.5FM and is now a new radio personality there. She is also the Founder of Out of The Shadows Outreach Ministry (non-profit), Founder and CEO of A Heart Pounding

Success CPR Mobile business and runs her small business endeavors, to include health and wellness, through Shirley LaTour Enterprises, LLC.

Her passion is helping women realize their full potential, through Christ alone. She started having "Coming Out of The Shadows" events August 2016 and later officially founded "Out of The Shadows Outreach Ministry" (O.O.T.S) June 2017. She is a former First Lady, having made it through a 16-year broken "Christian" marriage and divorce and she wants to let others know that divorce is NOT the end of the world but an opportunity for NEW LIFE! She has two wonderful children.

She is an avid volunteer in the surrounding communities and seeks to expand her reach around the world! With God, ALL things are possible. "To God Be the Glory!" shirleylatourenterprises.com or shirley@ shirleylatourenterprises.com to inquire about being a co-author, author or any of her services to the community.

TAMMIE MALDONADO was born and raised in California but has lived in Killeen, Texas for the past four years. She was addicted to drugs for twenty-four years before becoming set free. She is a mother of five and a grandmother of twelve.

Tammie finished school May of 2018 and received an Associate's Degree in Chemical Dependency Specialization. She is currently working as a substance abuse counselor at *Teach Them To Love Community Outreach (T3L)* in Killeen, TX where she has the opportunity to work with clients who are going through or have come out of the judicial system. Tammie's main focus is rehabilitation along with or in place of incarceration. She believes wholeheartedly that change is possible in anyone and that through reentry programs that include case management, guidance and love even those that have become institutionalized according to the world's standards can turn their lives around. Tammie plans to further her schooling in Social Work and to continue working in community outreach.

Contact Email: <u>freedomoutofbrokennness@gmail.com</u>

SHARON FINNEY is an Army veteran on a mission to encourage and inspire through writing, for growth and healing. She is the author of the memoir, Sweet Magnolia and co-author of Behind the Rank, Vol. 1, both of which are Amazon best sellers. After publishing Sweet Magnolia, she established the Magnolia M. Bradford Memorial Scholarship as a tribute to her late mother. Book sales helped to fund the first award in August 2018. Sharon's work has been featured in *Women Who Served* Magazine, the *Panama Cyberspace News*, and DIGEST THIS! Ministry Magazine and *The Pastor's Message*. She is a devoted wife and mother who enjoys spending time with her family and supporting charitable endeavors in her local community.

Sharon and her husband Lewis are the owners of the metro DC consulting firm, L&S Enterprise, LLC where they promote premarital counseling and marriage enrichment from a Christian perspective.

Learn more at www.LSEnterprise.org

CANDY L. MOSES was born in Frederick, Wisconsin on July 22, 1960, and currently resides in Killeen, Texas. She is currently working as a seamstress in her own business, "Ibesewingstuff".

Candy was ordained as an elder in 2003, under the leadership of Apostle Lorenzo Tucker of Reformation Church, INC. and has served in the ministry in some capacity since she was 14 years old. She currently serves on the ministerial staff at Jesus Name Apostolic Ministry in Copperas Cove, Texas where Elder David J. Davis Sr. is the Pastor.

She is a single mother of three adult children and eight grandchildren. She is a veteran of the U.S. Army and Reserves, and a retired high school teacher.

TAYLOR STEPHENS is a native of New Jersey who enlisted in the US Army after graduating high school in 1995. She began her professional education at Hawaii Pacific University earning an AS in Management in 2003 and BA in Justice Administration in 2005. She obtained her initial graduate degree at Webster University earning a Master of Human Resource Management in 2009. Later in pursuit of her calling she returned to graduate school earning a Master of Social Work from Monmouth University in 2014. Taylor is a Licensed Social Worker specializing in Substance Abuse, Traumatic Brain Injury, Suicide Prevention Intervention and Mental Health Disorders. She has volunteered in various communities across the country directly supported by outreach ministries. Her professional affiliations include: Alpha Delta Omega and Phi Alpha National Honor Societies, National Association of Social Workers and Monmouth

University Veterans Association. Taylor is the single mother of two wonderful teenage boys.

NOVICE MCDANIEL is married to her best friend, Bobby McDaniel. She is a faithful member of Christian House of Prayer in Killeen, TX. Novice is a fully licensed minister of the Gospel under Covenant Connections International and is a certified Christian life coach. She is the founder and owner of Divine Identity Christian Life Coaching & Consulting.

As a teacher of life in the Kingdom, her desire is to assist people in obtaining true balance in spirit, soul, and body; endeavoring to be a signpost, pointing people in the direction of Jesus Christ.

She has authored three books, "Lord of the Sabbath, Rest in Jesus," "Peace in the Storm," and "Declaring God's Decree, 31 Days of Scriptural Prayers & Confessions."

Novice is a veteran of the United States Army and she has embraced the call of God to herald the Gospel of Jesus Christ to all nations.

Email: divineid3@gmail.com

Phone: 254-629-7006

www.novicemcdanielministries.com

Facebook Pages: Novice McDaniel, and Encouragement Made Easier with Minister Novice

DR MONICA DEBRO, owner of Love Yourself to Life, is a leader who is transforming the lives of women through inspirational writings, events, and speaking engagements. She is the host and keynote speaker for The Elephant in the Room and the Love Yourself to Life conferences. Dr. Debro also hosts the Always Wear Your Tiara event in which women have received intimate breakthroughs in their personal lives.

She is a practicing Nurse Educator and Life Coach who engages in life-changing conversations. Her transparency allows her to be influential in helping others identify current concerns and develop specific and realistic action steps to reach their goals.

Dr. Debro is a member of the National Coalition Against Domestic Violence and has been a guest speaker at several domestic violence and community violence awareness conferences. She is the author of Broken Believer No More and Love Yourself to Life.

mdebro@forevershalom.com

www.loveyourselftolife.co

#Love2Life

ROXANNE ROBINSON was born and raised in "Motor City", Detroit, Michigan, known as Motown. She now resides in North Carolina with her three children (2008). Roxanne's passion for helping people led her into a career of real estate (licensed in NC & MI) and financial coaching. Roxanne has extensive banking and finance experience. She realized she had a strong connection with financial management when she opened her first bank account at 16 years old at NBD Bank and later began her career in banking. All of the learning has contributed to and prepared her for a successful business career. She belongs to Toastmasters International, a leader in communication and leadership development, which has contributed to her growth in public speaking and written communication. She holds an MBA in Strategic Management and a BBA in Marketing.

Roxanne enjoys reading, writing, planning and traveling.

Her favorite types of books are personal and professional development.

www.rmrobinsongroup.com

email: rmrobinsongroup@gmail.com

SANDI JOHNSON is a motivational speaker, vision & accountability coach. Her simple motto of "set a goal, achieve that goal and move on to the next goal" has been the driving factor in her success. Her life's goal is to merge her faith, gifts, passion, purpose and education to help others "Live Life on Purpose," which is the name of her social media broadcasts.

After 5 years of hosting vision board events, in 2018, "EnVision Your Life" where clients are inspired and coached to achieve their goals and life's purpose was birthed.

Additionally, Sandi has co-hosted "My Story, My Journey" Women's Retreat for the past 5 years. On occasion, she can be found co-hosting "You're Worth It" Radio Talk Show. Sandi speaks at educational institutes, retreats, conferences and workshops.

She is the mother of three adult children, Sydney, Kristen and Jonathan, and currently resides in Lewisville, Texas.

To learn more, visit www.sandidjohnson.com

SHONDA M. CURB was born in Arlington, TX in 1981. She served one tour in Iraq and one tour in Korea during her service in the US Army. In 2007, Shonda earned an associate's degree from Central Texas College before being honorably discharged from the military. Shonda went on to earn a BS in Religion from Liberty University in August 2012. Following this, Shonda began to work in the community with local assemblies and other pastoral committees to provide resources and informal consultation to married couples and families. Shonda went on to enter Liberty Baptist Theological Seminary in an effort to follow her calling towards Pastoral Counseling. She developed a love for spiritual integration and biblical studies during this time. Shonda finally earned a Master's of Divinity from Liberty in June 2015. In working with families, Shonda discerned a need for more in depth clinical practices, especially with regards to couples. She conferred a Masters in Marriage, Family, and Child Counseling from the University of Mary Hardin-Baylor in December 2017 to facilitate this need. Her journey with UMHB has cultivated a love for play, sand, and mindfulness interventions in therapy. She is joined on her journey by her husband and four children. She continues to work with people to encourage their pursuit towards wellness and living a life of active faith.

TRUENICE BRYANT-SHAW is a woman of many hats. She is a devoted mother of four, a worship leader, Radio Host, a Songwriter, a Youth Leader, but most importantly she is a woman after God's own heart. She is the founder of Truenice Shaw Ministries where her mission and endeavor is to reach the lost at any cost, and inspire however she can, for growth and healing. Using her God-Given gift to go forth in what she has been called to do in such a way that it would cause lost souls to be found, burdens to be lifted, hearts mended, yokes destroyed, and the crying out "What must I do to be Saved." Her prayer is for the people to ONLY see God at work through her.

You can keep up with Truenice Shaw Ministries through the different social media platforms.

Remember, it's only up from here.

ABOUT OUT OF THE SHADOWS OUTREACH MINISTRY (O.O.T.S.)

Out Of the Shadows (formerly named Coming Out of The Shadows) was first given to Shirley LaTour, Founder, as an assignment for healing. After the first event was held on August 13, 2016, she quickly realized that this was NOT just for her but discovered that many women need to "Come Out of The Shadows". This is a GOD ASSIGNMENT. Women struggle inwardly with many things. We hold up as champs on the outside but many are broken on the inside. There is so much to be said of women. Let us be VICTORIOUS, overcomers and women of faith who UNAPOLOGETICALLY walk out the assignment of God for our lives; whether at home, on the job, in business, or in ministry. Time for healing for women all over the world, starting right in Killeen, TX! WALK IT OUT!

The very thing God prompted Shirley to do two (2) years before divorce, helping other women break free of fear and everything holding them back from their God given purpose, broke her free! She is a firm believer that God can and will do the impossible in every area of life for those that truly believe His Word. The WORD HEALS,

NOT time. No more shall we live in the shadows!

Officially founded as a Non-Profit Organization June 2017, O.O.T.S. endeavors to minister to the needs of women everywhere, bringing hope for a brighter tomorrow.

The ministry serves women who have been held back from being their true selves and all they were predestined to do in this life, those searching for a better way of living, breaking free of self-doubt, hatred, fear and so much more that hinders our walk with Christ and others.

Next stop: Reaching men! We all have a purpose, sometimes hidden: buried under past hurt and pain.

O.O.T.S also aims to give scholarships to children of Single parent homes and foster children phasing out of the system.

O.O.T.S. is held quarterly in Killeen, weekly meet-ups, movies and study sessions are on various topics of interest to women. Follow OOTS on FB and on our website!

FB: www.facebook.com/OOTShadows

Website: www.ootshadow.org

Profits from the first 100 copies, whether on Amazon or in print, will be donated to Out of The Shadows Outreach Ministry and back into the local community.

Teach Them To Love Outreach Ministry, a local non-profit domestic violence shelter, will receive these funds.

NOW IT'S YOUR TURN

Discover the EXACT 3-step blueprint you need to become a bestselling author in 3 months.

Self-Publishing School helped me, and now I want them to help you with this FREE WEBINAR!

Even if you're busy, bad at writing, or don't know where to start, you CAN write a bestseller and build your best life.

With tools and experience across a variety niches and professions, Self-Publishing School is the only resource you need to

take your book to the finish line!

DON'T WAIT

Watch this FREE WEBINAR now, and

Say "YES" to becoming a bestseller:

https://xe172.isrefer.com/go/ affegwebinar/bookbrosinc7655

34892110R00093

Made in the USA
Middletown, DE
02 February 2019